BOBBIN LACE

BOBBIN LACE

A CONTEMPORARY APPROACH
BY BRIGITA FUHRMANN

WATSON-GUPTILL PUBLICATIONS/NEW YORK

Copyright © 1976 by Watson-Guptill Publications

First published 1976 in the United States and Canada by Watson-Guptill Publications
a division of Billboard Publications, Inc.
One Astor Plaza, New York, N.Y. 10036

Library of Congress Cataloging in Publication Data
Fuhrmann, Brigita.
  Bobbin Lace.
  Bibliography: p.
  Includes index.
  1. Bobbin lace. I. Title.
TT805.F83 1976   746.2'2   76-21855
ISBN 0-8230-0520-8

Manufactured in U.S.A.

First Printing, 1976

To Andy and Chrissy

ACKNOWLEDGMENTS

During the past several years while conducting workshops and classes in lacemaking, I have met a large number of dedicated and enthusiastic people who have shown a sincere interest in learning this art. It is because of their interest and expressed need for a manual of peasant lacemaking that I undertook the writing of this book, which would not have been possible without the help of some very wonderful people whom I should like to thank here.

In this type of book the photographs are as important as the text, and I consider myself fortunate to have found a professional photographer of the caliber of Howard J. Levitz. It was also my good fortune to have editors as cooperative and helpful as Jennifer Place and Ellen Zeifer.

I am deeply indebted to the following museum personnel for their prompt and helpful assistance: Jo Bidner, Volunteer, Costume and Textile Department, Brooklyn Museum; Elizabeth Ann Coleman, Curator, Costume and Textile Department, Brooklyn Museum; A. Nahlik, Head, Polish Textile History Museum; V. A. Pushkarev, Director, Leningrad Museum; Larry Salmon, Curator, Textile Department, Boston Museum of Fine Arts; Milton Sondy, Curator, Textile Department, Cooper-Hewitt Museum; Dr. Maria Taszycka, Curator of Textiles, National Museum in Cracow, Poland; and Barbara Teague, Textile Department, Metropolitan Museum of Art.

The following people offered much more than was asked of them, and I found them not only helpful but encouraging: Mary Ann Beinecke, President, Hoosuck Community Resources Corporation; Gertrude Biederman, teacher of lacemaking and author; David Manzella, Head, Graduate School, Rhode Island School of Design; Dr. Ema Markova, Czechoslovakian Textile Authority; and Esther Oldham, collector of fans and laces.

I also wish to thank the following lacemakers who were generous enough to send more work than I could include in this book: Emilie Frydecka, Elena Holeczy, Kaethe Kliot, Suzanne Lewis, Mary Lou Reichard, Jarmila Sikytova, Cindy Van Dine, Lydia Van Gelder, and Marie Vankova.

I am especially indebted to my parents, Josef and Marie Holler, to Alice Marcoux, Ruth Ginsberg-Place, and James Russell for the encouragement and support they gave me during the initial phases of this book. And to my husband, Bill, without whom this book might never have reached completion, I wish to express my most sincere appreciation.

CONTENTS

INTRODUCTION

Lacemaking was the last traditional textile technique to come into existence, and during the 16th, 17th, and 18th centuries, it developed into one of the most expressive art forms. Whether it was made by peasants in Eastern Europe or by professional lacemakers in the courts of Western Europe, it was prized for its intricacy, delicacy, and decorative richness by people all over the world. After over a century of obscurity, lace is enjoying a revival as more and more artists are intrigued by its creative possibilities.

Along with knotting, tatting, and needle lace, bobbin lace is classified as a true lace technique, since it is used predominantly to make openwork fabrics. Bobbin lace is made over a pattern attached to a firm pillow. The threads used to make the lace are wound on bobbins, and pins hold the lace in position while it is being made. Whether the finished lace is simple or complex, the procedure and technique is the same—the bobbins are crossed and twisted over each other in varying sequences to form a wide range of stitches. The richness of the lace depends upon how these stitches are used and how they are combined.

A Slovakian lacemaker from Turie Pole at work on her cylindrical pillow. Photo Jozef Vydra.

HISTORY

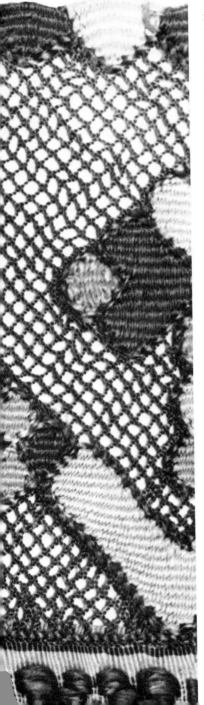

The development of the technique of bobbin lace is not well recorded, and a lot of the available information is founded on probability. The oldest specimens of lace have very rarely survived, and written descriptions are not always completely reliable. The first dependable recording of lace began with portrait painting, where details of clothing were accurately represented.

Knotting, plaiting, and weaving on a vertical warp all claim to be forerunners of bobbin lace—it is quite possible that in different countries bobbin lace developed from different techniques. Simple network and plaiting were almost universally known all over the world. Examples of these rudimentary laces have been found in excavations in Egypt, Peru, China, England, and Scandinavia. But the sophisticated technique of bobbin lace as we know it today did not appear until the latter part of the 15th century. The earliest form of bobbin lace was made with gold and silver threads, and these laces seem to have been haberdashery trims that later were developed into the intricate designs of the 16th century when fiber threads began to be used.

WESTERN EUROPE

There are two theories on the origin of bobbin lace in Western Europe—one that it originated in Italy in the 15th century, and the other that the technique was brought to Italy after being developed somewhere else, such as Dalmatia. (Dalmatia was the country to introduce bobbin lace to Eastern European countries and Russia.) In any case, the fact that lace made with bobbins existed in Italy in the 15th century is proved by written documents as well as by existing examples of lace.

From Italy the technique spread quickly to other countries. Since busy trade kept Italy in close contract with Flanders during the Renaissance period, the technique of lacemaking was carried there quickly. By the end of the 17th century, Flemish laces reached such a high degree of development that the origin of bobbin lace is very often ascribed to Flanders. Also in the 17th century, France—in addition to Italy, Holland, and Belgium—began to produce some of the most sophisticated laces, distinguished by their fineness and airiness. Colbert, a minister of Louis XIV, established the lacemaking industry in France and attracted the best designers.

Bobbin lace was already being made in England by the end of the 16th century, and it became widely spread very soon. English laces developed their own technical vocabulary—some types of lace such as Buckinghamshire and Honiton are still among the best known and most valuable.

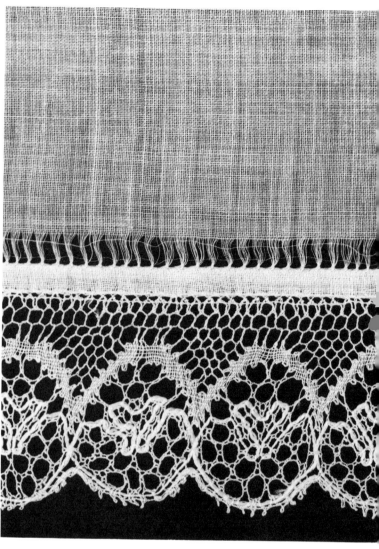

Fine Buckinghampshire edging made from linen thread in the 19th century. Collection of Brigita Fuhrmann.

16th century torah decorated in silver thread lace. Collection of the Jewish Museum in Prague, Czechoslovakia, photo and courtesy Jarmila Sykitova.

Motifs are skillfully combined in this wide edging of Brussels lace from the 19th century. Collection of Brigita Fuhrmann.

Spain, the European center of gold and silver laces, also produced some of the most beautifully colored silk laces as early as the end of the 16th century. The Scandinavian countries Sweden and Denmark have a long history of bobbin lacemaking too—the technique was probably brought there from Belgium. The technique of lacemaking spread widely in Scandinavia and has been used without any historical interruption up to the present. However, since the lace was made mainly by peasants for purely utilitarian purposes, Scandinavian lace never achieved a high degree of prominence.

During the middle of the 16th century bobbin lacemaking was introduced to the Saxony region of Germany by Barbara Uttmann, who came from Nuremberg to the mining town of Annaberg and taught lacemaking to the local people. The industry she established prospered for a long time and influenced lacemaking in all of Germany, Switzerland, and Bohemia.

The bobbin laces were first made predominantly by nuns for purely ecclesiastical purposes; but when Renaissance fashion adopted lace, it began to play a very important role in the clothing of the noble class and royalty. As the fashions of collars, ruffles, and veils changed, new and always finer styles of lace developed, and the demand for this subtle textile grew by leaps and bounds.

In the 17th century, Western European laces reached their most elaborate level of technical and esthetic development. With the 18th century came the most lavish large pieces of lace of highly complex designs. Silk became the most popular material, and it is from these times that the beautiful Spanish mantillas originated.

The French revolution was a

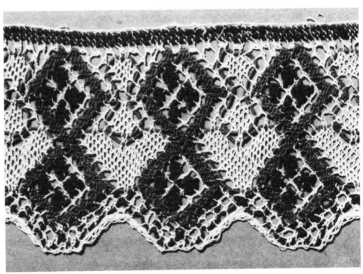

(Top) Three strips of lace were used to decorate the edge of this Russian wedding towel. The top insertion (closest to the towel) and the edging were made in straight lace with metallic threads, while the central strip was made in tape lace with green silk and a metallic gimp. Courtesy of the Brooklyn Museum, Brooklyn, New York, gift of Mary T. Harkness.

(Above) The scalloped edge on this 19th century border from Slovakia is made from white, green, and red cotton. Collection of Miss Ester Oldham, photo Bill Fuhrmann.

heavy blow to the lacemaking industry, since with the deterioration of the noble class the demand for elaborate lace became nearly nonexistent. From then on the fashion was simple, and the lavish laces ceased to exist. Even Napoleon I, who attempted to reintroduce the lace into fashion and commissioned designers and lacemakers to make many beautiful pieces, could not bring back elaborate laces.

The end of the handmade lace industry was, in effect, 1818, when the first bobbin net was produced by machine in France. Although the machine-made lace was considered an imitation at first and was not readily accepted, its lower price and availability quickly overcame the public's initial apprehension. Handmade lace became less and less in demand, even for very special occasions.

EASTERN EUROPE

Since bobbin lace was made primarily by professional lacemakers and was not practiced as a hobby, the technique would probably have been forgotten had it not been for the peasant lacemakers. While the professionals made the fancy lace styles marked for their originality and fragile beauty, peasants produced humble lace to decorate their daily clothes and costumes. Because the folk costumes were conservative and did not change with fashion, the designs and types of lace used on these costumes carried on a continuous tradition. This lace was of a consistently high though rather coarse quality.

Peasant lace developed in all European countries where bobbin lace was made. But in Eastern European countries and in Russia, where the peasant culture was much more prevalent than in the Western European countries, the bobbin lace made

(Top) This decorative border of a towel from the beginning of the 19th century was made by the tape lace technique in the city of Belozersk in the Novgorod region of Russia. Courtesy Gosudarstveniy Russkiy Muzey.

(Above) The straight lace technique was used to make this colorful silk towel border from Russia—it is complemented by equally colorful embroidery. Courtesy of the Brooklyn Museum, Brooklyn, New York, gift of Edward S. Harkness.

(Top) A red silk ribbon connects
the wide edging and the insertion in
this Russian straight lace border.
Courtesy of the Brooklyn Museum,
Brooklyn, New York, gift of Mary
T. Harkness.

(Above) Wide Russian border made
in tape lace with natural and red
linen. Courtesy of the Brooklyn
Museum, Brooklyn, New York.

by peasants for their own use developed into a highly sophisticated and technically outstanding craft with very unique and often very personal designs.

Bobbin lace was introduced to these countries from two sources—from Dalmatia, where the technique was carried through Yugoslavia to Slovakia and Russia, and from Germany and Flanders, where the technique was carried mainly to Bohemia and Poland. These two streams of influence crossed paths in many of these countries and developed into very distinct regional styles.

In Yugoslavia the first bobbin lacemaking centers were in Dalmatia and Crotia. Although Dalmatia is considered by some to be the cradle of the technique, the area did not develop into a world-renowned lacemaking center. Bobbin lace was and is still made in the Yugoslavian mining town of Idria, where presumably the first tape lace was made. (For this reason this type of lace is sometimes called Idria lace.) Bobbin lace is still made in other parts of Yugoslavia as well, and the technique is taught in a lacemaking school in Lublan founded in 1888.

In Russia bobbin-made gold and silver laces existed as early as the 15th century. These very simple, narrow trimmings—probably products of haberdashers—later developed into very rich and lavish laces decorating residences of knights, monastaries, and rich merchants, as well as the houses of the agricultural classes. Metallic lace was used on fur coats, on edgings for curtains, and even on trimmings for horse blankets. Bobbin lacemaking spread quickly, and the laces became an integral part of Russian folk art in the 17th century.

When Peter the Great tried to introduce the Western European type of lacemaking to Rus-

(Top) This wide Russian tape lace border is beautifully complemented by the fabric—embroidered in drawnwork and darning patterns—to which it is attached. Courtesy of the Brooklyn Museum, Brooklyn, New York, Ella C. Woodward Memorial Fund.

(Above) A wide edging from Russia made from natural linen in the 19th century. Collection of Brigita Fuhrmann.

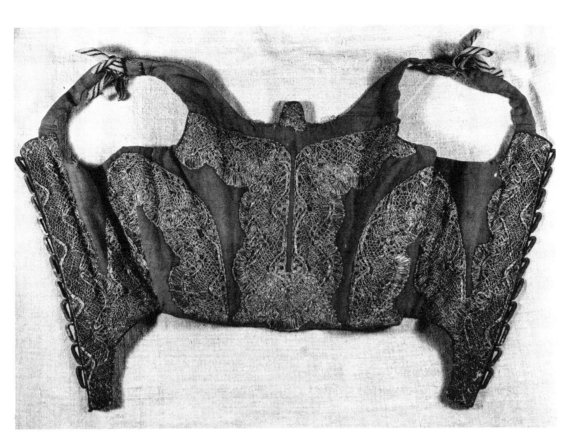

(Top) Lace made of gold thread lavishly decorates this woman's bodice from Slovakia. Collection of U.L.U.V. Bratislava, courtesy Ema Markova, photo S. Stepanek.

(Above) Many colors are used in this tape lace edging from the town of Bosace (Nove Mesto Nad Vahom region) in Slovakia. From the Archive of U.L.U.V. Uherske Hradiste, C.S.S.R., courtesy Ema Markova, photo M. Shotola.

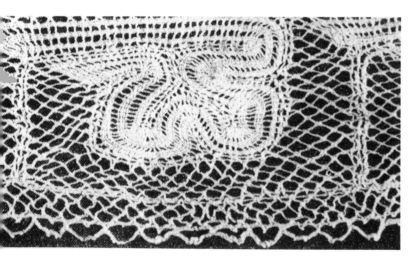

Three examples of tape lace edgings made in Poland in the 18th and 19th centuries. Collection of the National Museum in Cracov, photolab of Centralne Muzeum Wlokiennictwa.

sia in the 18th century, he only partially succeeded. A lacemaking school was established, and Russian lacemakers produced enough fine laces based on western designs to export them. But the peasant laces did not seem to be influenced by this foreign trend, and their designs continued in an uninterrupted development. These laces were integral parts of folk costumes and household linens. Although both straight and tape laces were made, the tape lace technique was the most popular—designs for this kind of lace achieved the most outstanding originality in Russia. For this reason tape lace is sometimes called Russian lace, although it was not invented in Russia nor was Russia the only country where tape lace was made. In Russia itself tape lace is called German lace, although it was not introduced there from Germany.

Russian folk costumes are very colorful and rich, and it is not unusual to find intricately woven and printed fabrics, embroidery, and lace all used to decorate a single costume. The lace was usually made out of bleached or natural linen with colored thread that related the lace to the rest of the colorful costume to which it was attached. The desire for color was so great that the lacemakers began to use colorful cotton threads with the linen—they used cotton thread because it accepted bright dyes much more readily than linen thread. The favorite color in Russian lace was red, although in the northern parts of the country it was often blue. Of course, there were always exceptions, and many beautiful laces combined the bleached and natural colors of linen with pink, blue, green, and brown silk.

Inspiration for Russian laces came from countries to the east

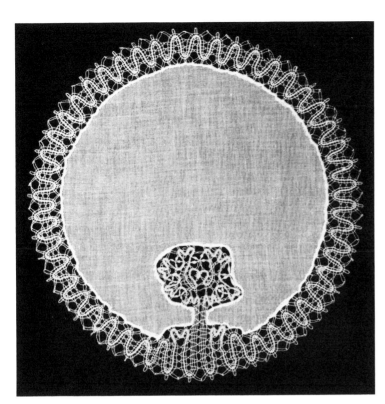

Tree of Life *by Brigita Fuhrmann, 11″/280mm in diameter. Circular wedding handkerchief—the cotton tape lace edging is attached to a linen fabric.*

(Below) Contemporary festive apron worked in both tape and straight lace and made in the U.S.S.R. Courtesy of the owner, Mrs. Mary Lou Reichard.

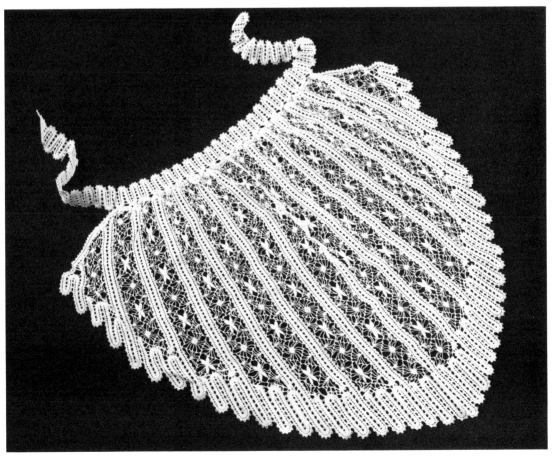

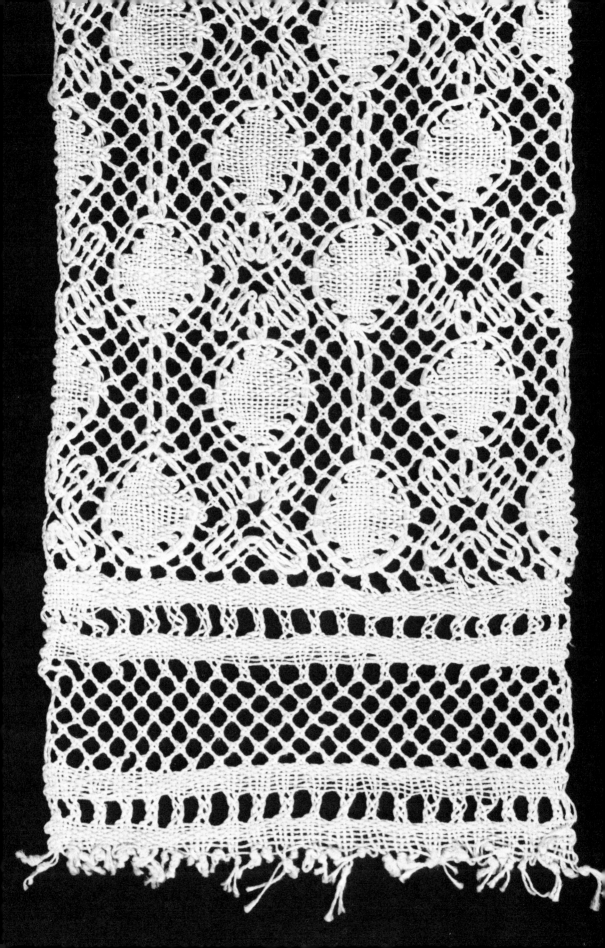

and south of Russia, and some designs of Turkish woven fabrics from the 16th and 17th centuries can be found in many Volgoda laces. The most common design elements in straight laces were the diamond and highly stylized female figures, although multicolored designs of stylized birds such as peacocks and trees, especially the tree of life, appear on very wide straight laces. Basically the same designs appear in tape laces, the tree being represented very often by a single blossom. The tapes were usually linen with ground worked in metallic or colored silk threads.

Several lacemaking centers developed in Russia, the biggest and oldest of which is Volgoda. Other well-known centers were Kirov, Michailovo, and Ryazan, each of which was distinguished for a unique characteristic. Kirov laces, for example, contained designs of flowers and other greenery, while laces produced in Michailovo were extremely colorful and gay and resembled embroidery.

Czechoslovakian lace was equally influenced by trends from both south and west of that country. While eastern Slovakia clearly reflects the influence from Yugoslavia, western Bohemia accepted bobbin lace trends from Belgium and from the nearby Saxony region in Germany. In 1642 in the Bohemian town of Vamberk, a Belgian lacemaker established a bobbin lace center that is still one of the most active lacemaking industries in Czechoslovakia. Bohemian laces were predominantly straight laces made with fine, white linen thread. Although many foreign influences can be found in the laces of Bohemia, this region developed its own unique style. The sequence later reversed itself, and Germany, Tyrol, Moravia, and Slovakia adopted ele-

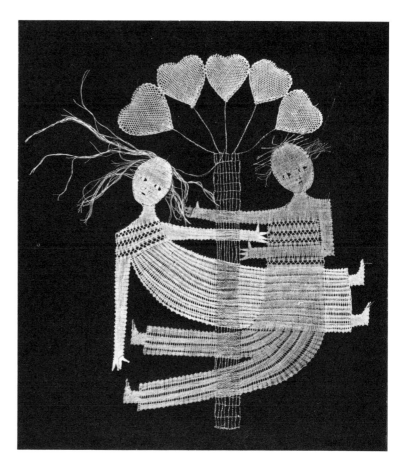

Wedding Congratulations *(Top) by Hana Kralova, 1961. A straight lace composition by a Czechoslovakian lacemaker now living in Israel. Courtesy Jarmila Sykitova.*

(Opposite page) Detail of a 20th-century Swedish lace using a traditional Scandinavian design worked in linen thread. Collection of Mrs. Margareta Grandin-Nettles.

White Birds *(Above) by Elena Holeczy, 7" x 14" / 180mm x 360mm, 1968. Tape lace composition in white and silver threads by a Slovakian lacemaker. Courtesy of the artist, photo S. Stepanek.*

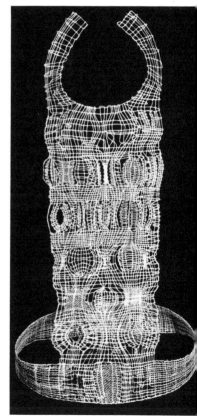

Omilienci (Above) by Elena Holeczy, 55″ x 61″ / 1400mm x
1550mm, 1969–70. Straight lace
composition in handspun hemp
and linen threads in natural colors
with gold metallic thread added.
Courtesy of the artist, photo Pavel
Janek.

(Left) Vest by Kaethe Kliot, 1974.
Courtesy of the artist, photo Jules
Kliot.

(Right) Waist-length necklace by
Marie Vankova, a Czechoslovakian
lacemaker, 1974. White linen and
golden metallic threads. Collection
of Museum of Applied Arts, Prague,
Czechoslovakia, courtesy of the
artist, photo Jan Syrovy.

(Opposite page) Necklace by Marie
Vankova, 1971. Black linen, golden
metalljc thread, and beads. Collection of the Lace Museum in Vamberk, C.S.S.R. Courtesy of the artist,
photo Jan Syrovy.

ments of Bohemian lace designs.

Slovakian laces are among the most original in their peasant designs and in their use of colorful threads. These laces, like those of Russia, display a wide range of colors to coordinate with the folk costumes and household linens. The first lacemaking centers in Slovakia were in mining regions like Banska Stiavnica and Kremnica. Later, peddlers carried the laces all through the country, and the agricultural class accepted them as an important part of their culture and started to produce the laces themselves. Each region developed its own characteristic designs; the laces of mining towns were usually white, fine, and precise, since they were made professionally for sale; the laces made by the farmers themselves were more colorful, coarse, and rustic.

Information about lacemaking in Poland does not appear before the 16th century. Some existing examples dating from the 16th and 17th centuries are very simple straight laces with designs of stylized flowers— mostly tulips. The first written facts concerning the production of lace in Poland date from 1777, when a lacemaking center was established in Grodno (now part of the U.S.S.R.) by a lacemaker from Brussels. In the 18th century lacemaking in Poland became very popular, and many beautiful laces were created for local use as well as for export. The lacemaking tradition was not interrupted even in the 19th century, when two lacemaking schools were established, the most important one of which was in the Silesia region. The majority of Polish laces are white, but some color schemes are worked into the ones designed in Slovakia.

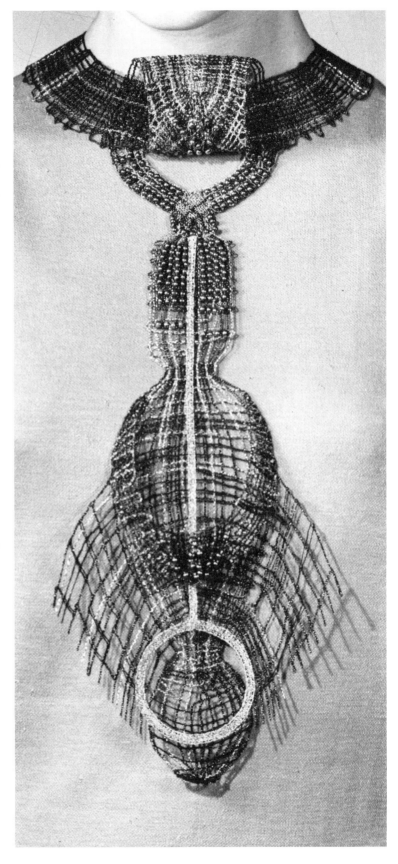

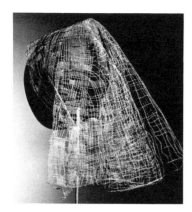

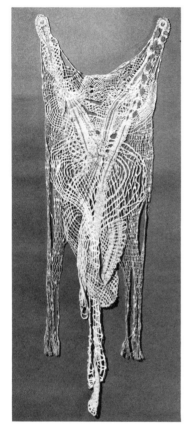

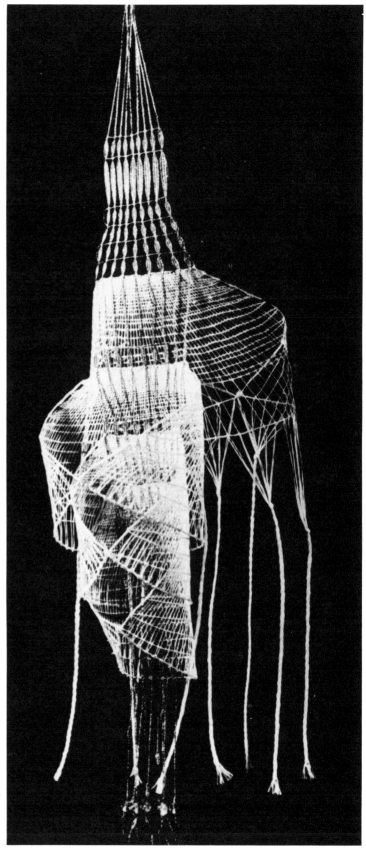

(Top) Festive veil by Marie Van-kova, 1968. Made entirely of golden and silver metallic threads with beads. Collection of Museum of Jewelry in Jablonec nad/nisou, C.S.S.R. Courtesy of the artist, photo Jan Syrovy.

Dolor (Above) by Brigita Fuhrmann, 1971. Wall hanging in red, brown, and natural linen.

(Right) Sculptural lace hanging by Emilie Frydecka. Made from white linen thread. Courtesy of the artist, photo V.S.U.P.

CONTEMPORARY LACEMAKING

It is quite evident that there is a renewed interest in lacemaking today by artists all over the world who wish to explore this intriguing textile technique. Lacemakers now form cooperatives to share ideas, information, sources of material, and outlets for their work. While some schools in Eastern and Western Europe have been offering courses in lacemaking for the last century, other schools all over the world are now expanding their art departments to include this technique.

While in the 16th, 17th, and 18th centuries, lace could usually be identified by unique characteristics of a country or region, today these distinctions are less defined. Instead, lace is becoming recognizable more by personal style than by national style. This is probably due to a number of factors, one of which is an ever-expanding communications system. A lace technique indigenous to a particular region is now accessible to a lacemaker thousands of miles away. Contemporary lacemakers not only have the widest selection of techniques available to them, but they also have an expanded variety of materials with which to experiment. The objects they make range from the tradtional edgings and insertions to entire pieces of clothing and large two and three-dimensional wall hangings.

It is almost impossible to imagine how something so rich and intricate, so open and delicate, and so seemingly complex as bobbin lace can be broken down into a few basic principles that can be mastered quite easily. But it is possible, and in the following chapters you will learn these principles and how they are used to form stitches and combinations of stitches. Once you become familiar with this essential information, you will be able to explore and experiment with bobbin lace and create laces of your own design. Your creations, whether small and humble or large and ambitious, will be your own expressive interpretation of this beautiful textile form.

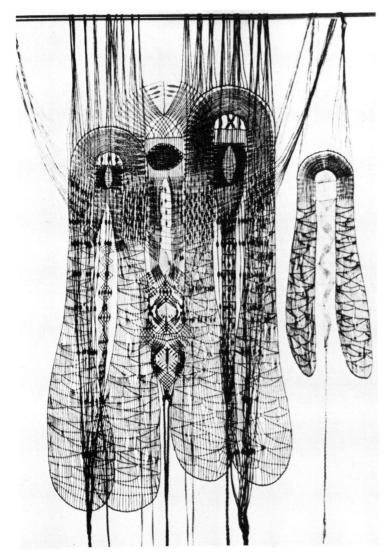

Black Angels by Emilie Frydecka. Straight lace wall hanging made with black and white linen threads. Courtesy of the artist, photo V.S.U.P.

TOOLS AND MATERIALS

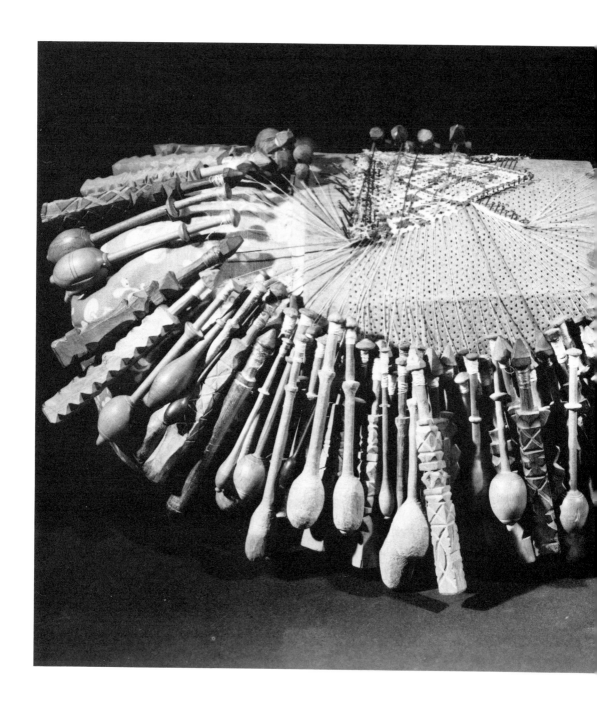

Lacemaking tools are simple and exquisite works of art in themselves (see Figure 1). In addition they are light and easily transported. In this section you will not only learn about them but you will also learn how to make many of them yourself. If you wish to purchase the tools, you may do so at a minimal cost. The materials you will need are also relatively inexpensive when compared to the worth of the finished lace.

TYPES OF PILLOWS

The cylindrical pillow and the flat cookie pillow are by far the most common pillows used by lacemakers in all lands. Nearly all other pillows are variations of these two types and were developed for specialized uses or in specific countries or regions. There are many types and forms of pillows, but I will describe only a few of the more common ones here.

Cylindrical Pillow. Historically, the cylindrical pillow was used in Germany, Russia, and Italy, but now it is used almost universally for making yard goods such as edgings and tapes.

Figure 1. *The beautiful bobbins being used to make this lace on a cylindrical pillow from Slovakia are hand-turned and hand-carved. Courtesy Dr. Ema Markova, Collection of U.L.U.V. Bratislava, Photo Pavel Janek.*

It is a cylindrical bag about 6″ to 8″/150mm to 205mm in diameter and 10″ to 12″/ 255mm to 305mm long, stuffed firmly with a material substantial enough to hold the shape of the pillow and soft enough to be penetrated by pins. Most of these pillows are solid, but some are hollow, resembling a muff (see Figure 2). The cylindrical shape allows the lace to be worked round and round continuously—when you have worked your way around the diameter of the pillow, you simply unpin the completed lace and keep going. Figure 3 shows a cylindrical pillow all set up— the hanging bobbins help create the proper tension on the threads.

Most likely, the first problem encountered by lacemakers who used these pillows was the tendency for the pillow to roll. They solved the problem by propping it up against a table leg, a sofa, or some other knee-high object, and lacemakers still do this today.

To bring the cylindrical pillow closer to the eye and to allow the lace to be worked even more comfortably, stands consisting of four wooden legs connected by wooden spindles were made for them (see Figure 4). These wooden legs and spindles usually were and still are made on a lathe. This framework serves as a cradle for the pillow, which when pushed into

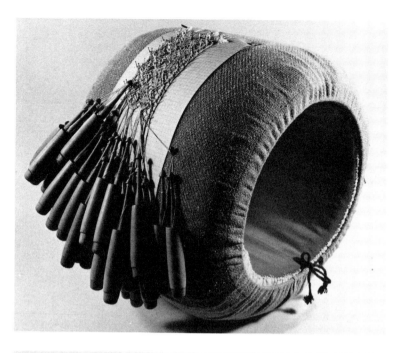

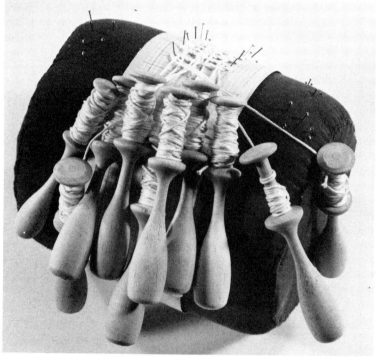

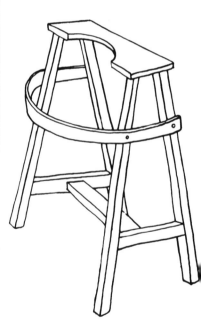

Figure 2. *(Top) Large-diameter cylindrical pillows are sometimes hollow. A weight is placed inside the cylinder to keep the pillow from rotating while you work the lace.*

Figure 3. *(Above) Small cylindrical pillow set up for working.*

Figure 4. *These two typical floor stands for holding cylindrical lace pillows—Italian on the top and English on the bottom—are two of the more common types in use today. Both of them are designed to allow the pillow to be supported in many different positions, increasing the flexibility of pillow movement.*

the stand rests well above the table top. As the lace progresses, you simply lift up the pillow and turn it—the stand allows for a greater flexibility of movement.

Cookie Pillow. The cookie pillow, designed for making motif laces, was also developed to allow a greater flexibility of pillow movement. Since the lace motif must be worked in all directions, the cookie pillow is a circular piece of wood covered by fabric and stuffed so the central portion is the highest section, sloping toward the edges. You work lace on the flat center portion and let the bobbins fall off the edges of the pillow (see Figure 5).

In order to tilt the lace toward you for better visibility and to make it easier to work, these pillows are set onto a little slanted box with a hole in the top that has a dowel protruding through it from the disc bottom. This way you can revolve the pillow to the proper working position. These boxes often come with a small drawer that can be used to hold bobbins, pins, completed lace, and perhaps covering cloths.

Spanish Pillow. The Spanish cylindrical pillow (see Figure 6) is only slightly larger in diameter than the smaller cylindrical pillow described above, but it is nearly three times as long. Originally it was made of straw bundled together with the ends squared off and covered with fabric. Thus the Spanish pillow used to be smaller in diameter at one end than it was at the other.

This pillow is usually accompanied by an adjustable floor stand that allows the pillow to be lowered, raised, and tilted backward and forward. Thus, even though the pillow is somewhat bulky, the stand allows you to place the work near you at the proper level. This pillow

Figure 5. *(Top) This typical cookie pillow is large enough in diameter to accommodate large laces while not permitting the bobbins to hang entirely off the pillow.*

Figure 6. *(Above) Many of the wide lace shawls, curtain edges, and table runners so popular in Russia had to be worked on a very large cylindrical pillow such as this Spanish pillow. The stand was widely used in Russia and other eastern European countries.*

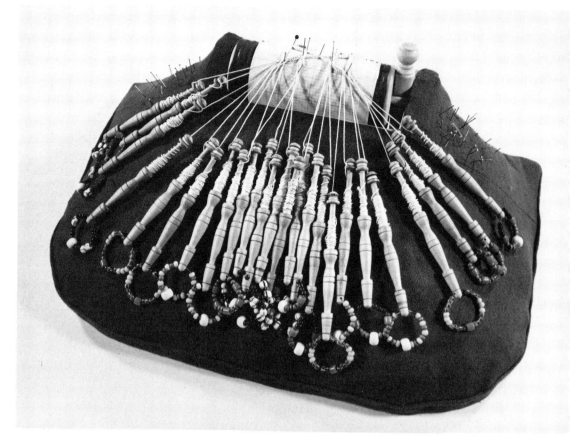

Figure 7. (Above) The small cylinder in this French mini-pillow turns on an axle. The wooden wedge on the right of the cylinder functions as a brake.

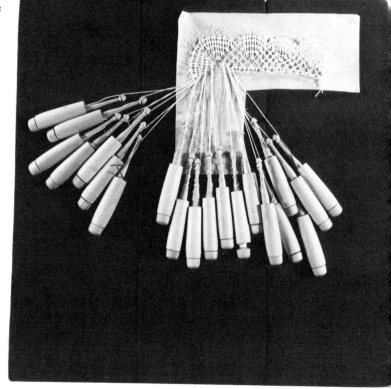

Figure 8. The lace being made on this Belgian segmented pillow just reached a corner. At that point, the upper middle pillow was removed and rotated 90° so the other half of the corner could be worked on without rotating the entire pillow. You can also use the three center pillows for making continuous lace by periodically removing the top pillow and sliding it into the position formerly held by the bottom pillow.

can also be used for larger works or several different works simultaneously.

French Mini-Pillow. The French mini-pillow, used in England and Belgium as well as in France, combines the features of the cylindrical pillow and the cookie pillow. The base can be round, oval, square, or rectangular, and, like the cookie pillow, it is padded least at the edges and builds up to a high point slightly to the rear of center. At this point is a well, fitted with a small cylindrical pillow where the lace is worked. You rotate the cylindrical pillow as the work proceeds, while the bobbins lie on the cookie (sloping) portion of the pillow (see Figure 7). Sometimes a little drawer in the back of the pillow holds the finished lace.

The variations developed for revolving and holding the pillow stationary while the lace is worked are numerous. They range from a snug fit in the well to axles, gears, and ratchets.

Belgian Segmented Pillow. Another variation of the cookie pillow is one used in Belgium to aid in the making of corners. The pillow is usually a square, divided into thirds. The two outside thirds are stationary, while the middle third is divided into three equal sections that can slide up and down between the two outside pads. All five sections are padded and covered. The lace is worked on the center three pillows only; when you reach a corner, you take the appropriate section out, turn it 90°, insert it back into the pillow, and complete the second half of the corner (see Figure 8).

You can easily construct both cylindrical pillows and cookie pillows at home, although there are some ready-made ones available from the suppliers listed in the back of this book.

Before I go into the specific instructions for making the various pillows, I am going to discuss the materials used.

PILLOWMAKING MATERIALS

All pillows must be made with cloth coverings and stuffing.

Cloth coverings. Every pillow has a covering directly over the stuffing. This covering should be a cotton or linen cloth dense enough to prevent the stuffing material from sifting through it and porous enough to accept pins. The seams in the cloth should be sewn with a tight stitch.

Another cloth of the same or a similar material is fitted over the inner one and secured by draw strings. This covering will be in direct contact with the lace and may be taken off for laundering. It should be a light, solid color, pleasing to the eye to reduce eye fatigue.

Stuffing. Pillow stuffing must be able to be packed firmly and hold its shape, be able to be penetrated easily by pins and yet hold them snugly, be non-corrosive to the pins, and be heavy enough to give the pillow sufficient substance. No one stuffing material that I know about has all of these qualities or properties. Therefore most stuffings are a combination of materials, such as fine sawdust mixed with sand and possibly some ground emery or carborundum. This last material was used historically to clean the pins as they were pushed in and pulled out of the pillow. If you use rustproof pins, this additional material is unnecessary. A heavy object such as a rock or a piece of metal is sometimes included in the center of the pillow stuffing (out of the reach of the pins) to add weight.

The stuffing used to wrap a cylindrical container may also

be purchased easily. Cotton batting, felt, a closely woven towel, and the matted pad used under carpets are all satisfactory either by themselves or in combination. The last material is perhaps the cheapest, as carpet companies throw away scraps of more than adequate size to make lace pillows.

Inner-Cores for Cylinders. Frozen juice cans make an ideal inner-core for the French mini-pillow. Other round cans and round cardboard containers—such as those used to package salt, hot cereals, and ice cream (for big hollow pillows)—make perfectly adequate inner-cores for the larger cylindrical pillows.

HOW TO MAKE PILLOWS

There are many ways to make pillows, and I will show you how to make the basic ones mentioned above.

Cylindrical Pillow Made with Fabric and Stuffing. One way to make a cylindrical pillow about 6″/ 150mm in diameter and 10″/ 255mm long is to sew a rectangular piece of fabric 11″ x 20″/280mm x 510mm (which includes a ½″/15mm seam allowance all around) together with two circular pieces of fabric 7″/ 180mm in diameter (again allowing for a ½″/15mm seam all around). To do this, first sew the 11″/280mm sides of the rectangular piece together, by hand or by machine, leaving—as always—a ½″/ 15mm seam. Then attach one 7″/180mm disk to one end of this cylinder. Stuff the cylinder compactly, and sew the other 7″/180mm disk to the open end of the cylinder to complete the pillow (see Figure 9).

To make the outer cover, cut a piece of fabric 15″ x 20″/ 380mm x 510mm. Sew a ½″/ 15mm hem on the two shorter sides. Next, sew a ½″/15mm

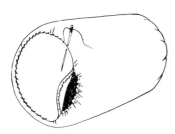

Figure 9. *After the cylindrical pillow has been firmly stuffed, you must sew the second circular piece of fabric to the open end by hand to complete the pillow. Notice the ½″/15mm seam of the disk tucked under the surface.*

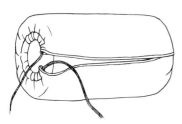

Figure 10. *The outer protective cover of the cylindrical pillow is large enough to allow a slight overlapping of edges and is drawn together and tied on both ends with drawstrings.*

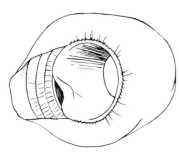

Figure 11. *The final step in making a hollow cylindrical pillow is to cover the inner core and padding with cylinders of fabric, which are then sewn together at the ends of the openings.*

hem on the two longer sides, leaving the ends open so you can run a drawstring through the hem. Wrap this fabric around the pillow, and draw and tie the two drawstrings on either end (see Figure 10). This completes the pillow and it is now ready to go.

Cylindrical Pillow Made with a Cylindrical Form. Another way to make a cylindrical pillow is to begin with a cylindrical form, such as an orange juice can or a cardboard container. Fill the can or container with gravel or sand to add weight if you like, or leave the cylinder open to produce a hollow pillow. Then wrap the cylinder with layers of stuffing material (see Stuffing above) until the stuffing is about an inch thick. This should be enough to prevent the pins from striking the cylinder wall, which could be destructive to the pins if the cylinder were a metal can.

Next, sew a cover over the stuffing, compressing it as much as possible, and attach two circular disks of fabric, one on each end. If you wish to make the pillow hollow, however, the cover sewn over the padding need only be about 1½″/40mm longer than the cylinder on either end. Line the inside wall of the cylinder with fabric, fold the extra 1½″/40mm on both sides over the edge, and sew the fabrics together (see Figure 11). You could put a weight in the hollow space to keep the cylinder from moving while you work the lace.

Cookie Pillow. The cookie pillow can be made several ways, but probably the best and simplest way is to buy or cut out a disk of wood (preferably plywood ½″/15mm thick or thicker) 16″ to 20″/405mm to 510mm in diameter. Then, cut a circular piece of fabric with a diameter equal to the diameter

Figure 12. *After stuffing the cookie pillow sufficiently through the small opening on the side, tack the remainder of the top fabric on the underside of the wooden base in regular pleats.*

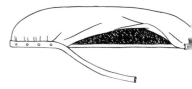

Figure 13. *If you want to, you can tack a tape edging to the edge of the wooden disk over the cover fabric for protection.*

of the disk *plus* twice the thickness of the disk *plus* 4″/100mm. Sounds complex doesn't it? Let me give you an example. If your disk is ½″/15mm thick and 16″/405mm in diameter, your fabric would be 21″/535mm in diameter.

Next, tack the border of the fabric along the bottom edge of the wooden disk. Since the diameter of the fabric is larger than that of the disk, you will have to gather the fabric evenly while tacking it down.

Leave about 12″/305mm of fabric untacked so you can stuff the pillow. Then arrange the stuffing so the pillow is highest in the center portion and slopes down at the edges. When the entire pillow is stuffed, tack the remaining fabric to the bottom of the disk (see Figure 12). In addition to this tacking, you may want to place a strip of fabric edging along the edge of the disk and tack it in place, but this is optional (see Figure 13).

Spanish Pillow. The long Spanish pillow is made in the same way as the cylindrical pillow with fabric and stuffing, except that the dimensions are different. Its typical size is 8″/205mm in diameter by 26″ to 30″/660mm to 715mm long. After you make the cylindrical bag that will hold the stuffing, you can add rigidity and help the pillow hold its shape better by making a wooden support to go inside with the stuffing. To make the structure, nail a plywood disk 8″/205mm in diameter and ¼″/7mm thick to one end of a dowel ¾″/20mm in diameter and about ¾″/20mm shorter than the pillow. Slide the dowel with the disk nailed to it into the cylindrical bag (see Figure 14) until the disk rests flat on the bottom. Stuff the pillow firmly to the top, nail a second disk 8″/205mm in diameter and ¼″/7mm thick to the end of the dowel (see Figure 15), and

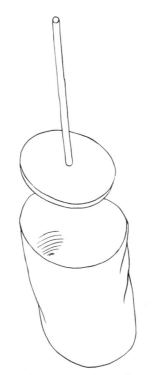

Figure 14. *To give structural support to the Spanish-pillow, slide a dowel with a wooden disk nailed to one end into the long cylindrical bag until the disk rests on the bottom of the bag.*

Figure 15. *After you have stuffed the Spanish pillow firmly to the top, nail the second disk to the other end of the dowel.*

sew the second circular piece of fabric to the end of the cylindrical bag. Please note that making this wooden structure to give the pillow more strength is an optional step.

French Mini-Pillow. Making the French mini-pillow requires more involved woodwork than the other pillows, but I will describe its construction briefly here. For convenience, let's use a board 18″/455mm square. First, construct an open wooden box 6″ x 7½″ x 5″/150mm x 190mm x 125mm (see Figure 16). Fasten this to the base in its proper location, referring to the diagram. Next, fit a fabric covering over the whole form (see Figure 7), hem the outside edge, and tack the cloth to the sides of the box and to the underside of the board. Don't tack the back until the pillow is firmly stuffed.

The core of the small pillow that fits into the box could be made from wood, or you might find a commercial container just the right size. For the box with the dimensions given above, the pillow should be about 3″/75mm in diameter and about 6″/150mm long. Place a dowel ⅜″/10mm in diameter and 8″/205mm long firmly through the center of this container. You may wish to fill the container with sand and gravel to add weight and give the pillow firmness. Wrap stuffing around the outside of the container until the pillow is 4¾″/120mm in diameter. Place a cover over this just as you would for the cylindrical pillow made with a cylindrical form. When you are finished, place the pillow with the dowel protruding from either end in the grooves at the end of the box and screw the cover pieces on (see Figure 16 for the shape of the cover pieces). The only other thing that is needed is a small wedge to place between the box and the pillow to keep it from turn-

Figure 16. *The basic parts of the French mini-pillow, from the bottom: baseboard, box in which the pillow will sit, pillow, and cover pieces that hold down the pillow. The box is fastened to the baseboard to the rear of center.*

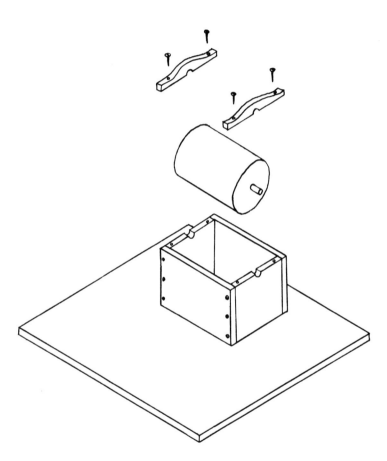

ing. The wedge in Figure 7, for example, has a lathe-turned top for a handle.

An easier way to achieve the same results with less carpentry is to make the cylinder without the dowel, the box without the grooves, and the pillow without the cover plates. You would secure the box in the same position on the platform, tack the cloth on, and stuff the pillow in the same way. The cylinder is made the same way but without the dowel through the center. This time, though, you would wrap the cylinder with stuffing to a diameter of slightly over 5″/125mm, so after you cover it with cloth and push it into the box, it wedges itself. To use this pillow, merely lift it out and turn as needed.

Belgian Segmented Pillow. The segmented Belgian pillow is quite simple to construct, but because of its highly specialized use, only the more advanced lacemaker may have a need for it. You will need a baseboard 18″/455mm square of (preferably) ½″/15mm plywood, two pieces of the same plywood 6″ x 18″/ 150mm x 455mm, and three pieces 6″ x 6″/150mm x 150mm. Pad all five pieces individually with about a 1″/25mm thickness of padding (stuffing material). Be sure that the three smaller pillows are padded to an even height; the two 6″ x 18″/ 150mm x 455mm pieces may be sloped to one long edge, although this slope is not necessary. Then cover the pieces individually, tacking the cloth to the underside of the board. Position the pillows on the baseboard so they are snug, and screw the two larger (outer) ones to the bottom board from underneath. The three smaller middle pillows should be able to slide between the two outer pillows with some resistance.

Specially Shaped Pillows. Specially shaped pillows and their use represent a possible realm of lacemaking for which an entire book could be written. While cylindrical and cookie pillows were historically the most commonly used because a flat lace was desired, oddly shaped pillows are in demand today to make laces with a three-dimensional shape. An umbrella provides a framework structure for a pillow in Figure 17. The frame was locked open, a fabric sewn all over the outside, the shape stuffed to form the pillow, and the pattern pinned to the outside and taped. The lace is being worked directly over the pattern in this figure. When completed, the lace, pattern, fabric, and stuffing will all be removed, and the lace will be attached to the framework structure to complete the parasol.

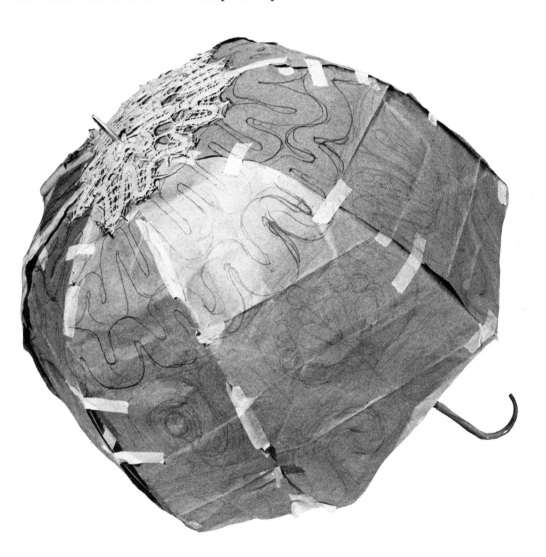

Figure 17. A parasol frame serves as a specially shaped pillow for lace worked on a pattern attached directly to the outside of the stuffed frame.

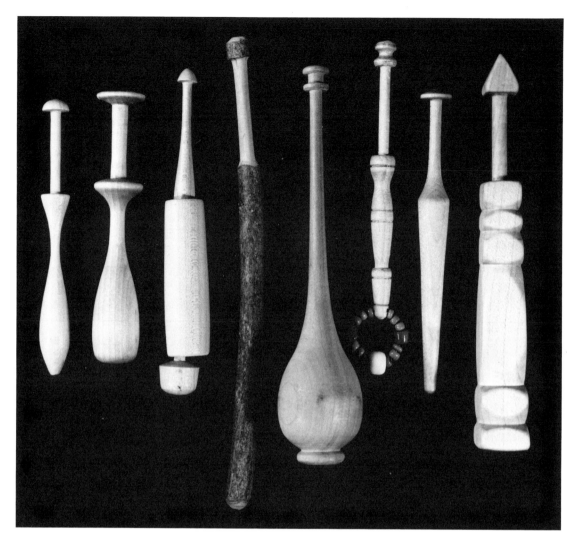

Figure 18. *Some of the more common bobbins used today (from left to right): Danish bobbin, widely used in the U.S.; Swedish bobbin designed to hold a large amount of thread; Viennese hooded bobbin; twig bobbin, hand carved from a lilac twig with bark remaining; Belgian or French bobbin with bulbuous handle; English bobbin with spangle; Russian bobbin from Volgoda region with pointed handle especially designed to perform crochetage; and hand-carved Slovakian bobbin.*

BOBBINS

Bobbins are the tools upon which each thread is wound—the lacemaker handles them in the process of crossing and twisting to create lace (see Figure 18). It is the one tool of the lacemakers trade that lends itself to creative expression by the craftsmen who make them. There are bobbins made of ivory, bone, all kinds of wood, ceramic, and glass. They have been whittled and carved, turned on a lathe, fabricated, and blown. They have been inlaid with paste, paint, metals, and even semi-precious stones. Inscriptions as ambitious as *The Lord's Prayer* have been inscribed into them. In fact, the number of variations among bobbins is so numerous that entire books have been written on bobbins alone.

Basic Parts and Functions. The three main functions of the bobbin are: (1) to store an ample amount of each thread to work with; (2) to keep the threads from becoming tangled; and (3) to add weight to the threads, which places the necessary amount of tension on the lace. Bobbins are designed to fulfill these functions. The shank (see Figure 19), the thin portion of the bobbin between the head and the handle, is where the supply of thread is wound for making the lace. On some bobbins the shank is very defined, while on others it is difficult to determine where the shank ends and the handle begins. In any case, the shank represents the upper half of the bobbin.

All bobbins have some sort of head. It is wider than the shank portion to keep the thread from slipping off the end of the bobbin. The slip-knot rests just under the head or, in the case of the grooved head, in the groove. The handle is the portion of the bobbin that varies the most as it is in direct contact with the worker. This is not to say that the comfort of the handle is the main factor in determining its form, but it is a consideration. More important is the weight factor, and its determination is based on the type of lace to be done and on what pillow the lace is to be made on.

Lace that is going to be made on a cylindrical pillow requires bobbins with handles that are not too heavy, since they will hang down freely. When the lace is made on a cookie pillow, the bobbins lay more horizontally, and thus a heavier handle is needed. To add weight, some bobbins are made uniformly larger in diameter; some are made with a large bulbous form at the end of the handle; some have a ring of beads attached to the end of their handles; and still others, called thumpers, have grooves cut or filed in the handle where lead or pewter is poured in.

The Viennese bobbin (see Figure 18), developed to hold thicker thread wound

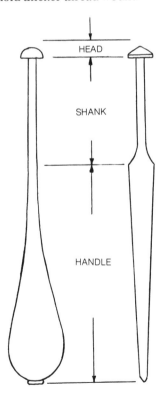

Figure 19. *Profiles of two different bobbins illustrating the three basic parts of all lace bobbins: the head, shank, and handle.*

directly on the handle portion of the bobbin, has a specially fitted wooden hood placed over the thread. The thread and hood give weight to the handle, and the hood protects the thread from dirt while it is being used.

Bobbins with pointed handles are used for making laces that require a good deal of crochetage, or sewing, in which the bobbin has to pass through a loop of thread, handle first.

The pillow loaded with bobbins in Figure 1 is amazing not only in the great number of bobbins but also in their decorative qualities and in the variety of types and forms. Although there are basic requirements that bobbins have to fulfill, the varieties in shape and esthetics may be endless. In all cases, though, bobbins are carefully chosen according to the thickness of thread to be used, the amount of sewing they will have to do, how much thread must be stored on them, and how comfortable they are to use.

HOW TO MAKE BOBBINS

If you would like to try making your own bobbins, there are a few ways to do it. The first possibility would be to find objects already in existence, such as clothespins, which could be used as bobbins temporarily and fairly adequately.

Your next choice would be to make some bobbins with a minimum of tools and machinery. Quite successful bobbins can be made from twigs—in fact, original Russian bobbins were made from twigs, bark included. The shank portion was simply whittled in with a knife. I made the bobbin fourth from the left in Figure 18 from a lilac twig. After I carved the shank portion, I sanded the bobbin taking care to round the edges. Then I sealed it with a coat of shellac, though I could have used varnish or a coat or two of boiled linseed oil rubbed in. This bobbin works very well on a cylindrical pillow.

Finally, the most professional way to make bobbins is to turn them or have them turned on a wood lathe.

Whether you are making bobbins from twigs or turning them on the lathe, they should be made from a hardwood such as maple, birch, walnut, cherry, or the like. Hardwoods are stronger and heavier than softwoods, and they sand to a smoother finish. All wooden bobbins should be sealed with at least one coat of shellac, varnish, or boiled linseed oil and allowed to dry thoroughly before using. Other materials such as ivory, bone, and plastic have been used—experiment with these materials and others if you like. Just keep the basic principles in mind when you make them.

BOBBIN WINDERS

I will discuss winding bobbins by hand in the next section. Until you begin doing a lot of lace, this is probably how you will wind bobbins. But if you find that you are winding bobbins constantly, you may want to invest in a bobbin winder. (See *Supplies and Suppliers* at the end of the book for where to buy bobbin winders.) One type of bobbin winder is operated by a hand crank—because of its gears, this machine turns the bobbin rapidly with little effort. Electric winders, of course, eliminate the need to crank by bin and The most critical area in the design of these winders is the bobbin-holding mechanism. It should be adjustable in order to accommodate all shapes and sizes of bobbins, and it should support both ends of the bobbin.

PINS

You would think that nearly any pin would serve adequately to hold lace that is in the process of being made. This may be true, but in the long run there are certain pins that have been proven to work better than others. There are several factors to consider when selecting pins: they should be of a material or finish that does not rust, since this would discolor the lace; they

should be strong enough to withstand the tendency to bend; and they should be shaped so they can penetrate the pillow easily.

Brass pins have been used in the past to overcome the rust problem, but they were too soft to be practical. Steel pins were used with pillows whose stuffing contained emery—the emery cleaned the pins as they were being used. Most straight pins you can buy today are either nickel-plated or made rustproof in some other way, and these are the pins you should use. The ones about 1″/25mm long seem to be satisfactory.

Pins with plastic heads are also useful because they are very thin and strong and penetrate the pillow easily. The larger head makes pushing them into the pillow easier on the fingers, but it also limits their use to lace made with thicker thread.

T-pins, about 1″/25mm long and nickel-plated, are also very useful for lace made of thicker thread. Hat pins, from 2″ to 3″/50mm to 75mm long, are ideal for holding groups of bobbins out of the way of the lace being worked on. All of these pins are easy enough to find in any store that carries sewing supplies.

THREADS

The time required to make lace is constant regardless of the quality of the materials used. And since the cost of the material used to make a lace represents only a fraction of its final worth, it is wise to use only the best quality material. The thread you select will depend, as it has in the past, on the function of the lace, the qualities it should possess, and the range of materials available.

You will want to consider a number of factors when designing your lace, whether it be a small edging for a piece of clothing, personal and household linens, or a wall hanging. How much wear will the lace be subjected to? Will it be laundered often? Is the lace going to

come in contact with the skin? Will it be exposed for long periods of time to direct sunlight? Answers to these and other questions will guide you in your search for the proper material to use. Linen, wool, silk, cotton, manmade fibers, and metallic threads provide the lacemaker with an ample variety of materials to fill these needs.

Linen Thread. Linen is the thread used most often in lacemaking. It comes in a wide selection of thicknesses and colors, is strong and durable, and is easily worked. A linen lace wears well, has a beautifully smooth finish, and retains its stiffness and body after an infinite number of launderings.

Wool Thread. Wool thread has been used very successfully, especially in peasant laces. The most suitable types of wool thread to use in lacemaking are those used in needlepoint, as they are of a very high quality and come in a wide variety of colors and thicknesses. For laces done in a larger scale, handspun wool provides a soft effect that is nearly unmatched by any other material. Wool is valued for its warmth and wearing qualities, and for this reason it is used in clothing articles. One factor to be aware of when designing laces to be made from wool is that the lace contracts (approximately 5%–10%) to a smaller size when it is unpinned from the pillow.

Silk Thread. Silk laces have the distinctive quality of being soft enough to fall into flowing pleats while having enough body to hold their shape beautifully. Silk is strong and wears well, although the laces made from silk are rather delicate. Silk comes in a wide assortment of colors and is often used in its rich, natural creamy color.

Cotton Thread. Cotton in its mercerized form is sometimes used in lacemaking. It is readily available in a wide variety of colors and thicknesses, wears well, and launders easily. The most common objection to cotton is that it produces a rather flimsy lace that needs starching after each laundering.

Manmade Fibers. Manmade fibers provide an interesting medium to explore for possible use in lacemaking. In the past they have been used only in conjunction with other lacemaking materials. Acrylics, for example, with many of the same qualities as wool, do not itch or shrink the way wool does, and they can be laundered more easily. Threads made of nylon and rayon are very beautiful and provide an interesting effect. The main disadvantage with these fibers is that they are very slippery, which makes tying knots nearly impossible, and they produce laces that soon lose their shape. Manmade fibers should be avoided by the beginning lacemaker, but they should certainly be experimented with by the experienced lacemaker.

Metallic Thread and Wire. Lace made with metallic thread or metal wire is, as you can expect, quite different from lace made with any other type of material. Metallic thread is produced by spiraling a thin and narrow flat ribbon of a pure metal such as gold, silver, copper, or aluminum around a cotton or silk thread core (see Figure 20). Metallic thread also comes in plied form. The plys may consist of two or more of these metallic threads or a combination of metallic thread and nonmetallic thread. Sometimes several metallic threads are braided together to form a flat ribbon called a ribbonette, which may also be used effectively for making lace.

The core of cotton or silk gives the metallic thread structure, body, and strength. The metals are used in their pure state and hence are soft, flexible, and not very strong. The core permits a thinner ribbon of metal to be used, giving the entire thread maximum flexibility at minimum cost. Even when

Figure 20. *A metallic thread is constructed by spiraling a flat wire around a fiber core.*

the metal is combined with the core, the thread is quite costly, and, as a result, plastics have been substituted for metal. The better ones are very effective and easy to work with.

Another advantage plastic has over some of the metals is that it does not tarnish. Pure gold and silver, like the plastics, do not tarnish, but karat gold, sterling silver, copper, and aluminum do. Because of this and the fact that metallic laces do not wear especially well and are nearly impossible to launder, metallic thread is used mainly for special decorative effects on clothing and uniforms. This should not discourage you from trying it—just use it with discretion.

Round wire may also be used for making lace, though you must be careful when you select the type of metal wire to be used. The best metals to use are gold, silver, or copper in its pure state. I have found that the copper wire used to rewind electrical motors is coated with a finish for which I could find no solvent—which makes it tarnish-proof. This finish also gives the copper wire a purple to orange color range.

Thin wires, from 22 gauge to 30 gauge, work the best, though the thicker wires, such as 20 gauge to 16 gauge, can be used as gimps. If the thicker wires are used as gimps, they are used in a passive role. Lace made with thin wire is amazingly flexible and supple, but when the wire has to be knotted, the ends are rather sharp. You can try to work the ends into the lace or plan to have no knots at all.

Round-wire lace has not, to my knowledge, been very widely explored, and the possibilities are exciting. For one thing, it has three-dimensional possibilities—the stiffness of the wire would become not only a decorative but also a structural element. The thicker wires might also be used with non-metal threads to produce a three-dimensional lace or to give shaped lace added rigidity.

BASIC TECHNIQUES

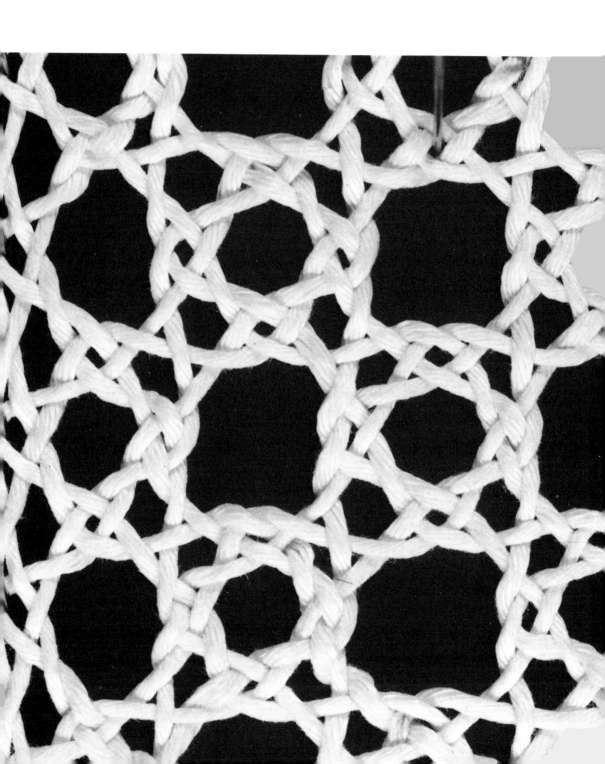

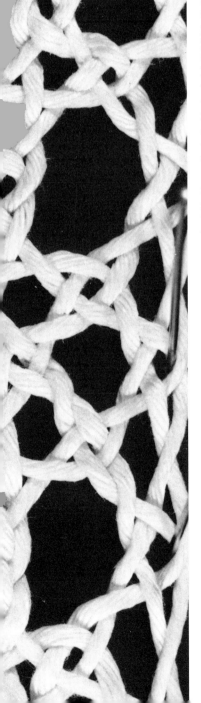

Bobbin lace is worked on a padded pillow fitted with a paper pattern (see Figure 1). To begin your lace, you insert pins into the beginning of the pattern and loop the pairs of bobbins wound with thread over them. You then pass the bobbins back and forth from one hand to the other, twisting and plaiting the threads into an intricate meshwork.

As the threads cross and move from one place to another, they follow the pattern beneath the work. As the work progresses, you pierce more pins through the pattern into the pillow to keep the threads in place. You should not remove the pins from the beginning of the work until you have completed several inches of newly pinned lace. After the lacework is completed, you tie and cut all the threads and remove the last pins to free the lace so it can be lifted from the pillow.

DRAFTING PATTERNS

One of the first things you should do before beginning a lace piece is to draft a pattern. The pattern is basically a schematic drawing of the lace including symbols of the stitches to be made, the places where the pins need to be inserted, and the overall shape the lace will assume.

All the patterns included in this book are complete, with indications of all pinholes and

symbols of stitches—and these symbols are stylizations showing only the most important elements of each stitch. By doing the exercises, you become familiar with this symbolic language, which enables you to design your own pattern complete with symbols. The more experienced you become, the less detailed your pattern has to be, and the more freedom you have to design spontaneously as the lace progresses.

Graph Paper. To achieve a uniform spacing of stitches throughout a piece of lace, the drafts are very often drawn on graph paper divided horizontally and vertically into a certain number of squares per inch or per centimeter. You can either buy graph paper, or, if you need a special size, you can draw your own.

Choosing the appropriate graph paper for a particular lace is not altogether an arbitrary decision. The major factor affecting this choice is the relationship between the size of the thread and the spacing of the stitches. If the threads are too crowded, the lace will be tough to the touch and will not have a lacy appearance. If the threads are spaced too far apart, the final lace will be flimsy and will lose its shape. One of the best ways to determine which graph paper to use is to do a small sample of lace using the same design on different density

Figure 1. *This small cylindrical pillow, dressed with a pattern, shows a partially completed lace being worked with hand-turned bobbins. Courtesy of Dr. Ema Markova, collection of National Museum in Martin, C.S.S.R., photo Jan Denev.*

graph papers with the thread you want to use. When your lace looks lacy and feels soft, but isn't too loose, you have the right size paper.

Another process for which graph paper is helpful is that of increasing or decreasing the scale of a lace pattern. The thread, of course, would have to be thicker or thinner accordingly. See Figures 2, 3, and 4 for an illustration of the same pattern on two different sizes of graph paper and the laces made from both patterns.

Transferring Patterns. Once you have your pattern on graph paper or on a piece of plain paper, you can tape it to a more rigid material, such as construction paper, and attach it to the pillow. Or you can draw the pattern directly onto the con-

struction paper or a similar paper—the paper should be stiff enough not to get pulled out of shape or folded by the tension of the lace but be easily penetrable by the pins. Whatever you do, though, always remember to draw the pattern with permanent, nonsmearing ink.

Many laces are reversible, but some have a right and a wrong side because of the design or because the lace requires that many knots be made on the wrong side. In these cases, drawings done on tracing paper can save time. Just pin the pattern to the pillow face down— you will be able to see it through the tracing paper—and work the lace from the back. When you unpin the lace, simply turn it over to see the right side.

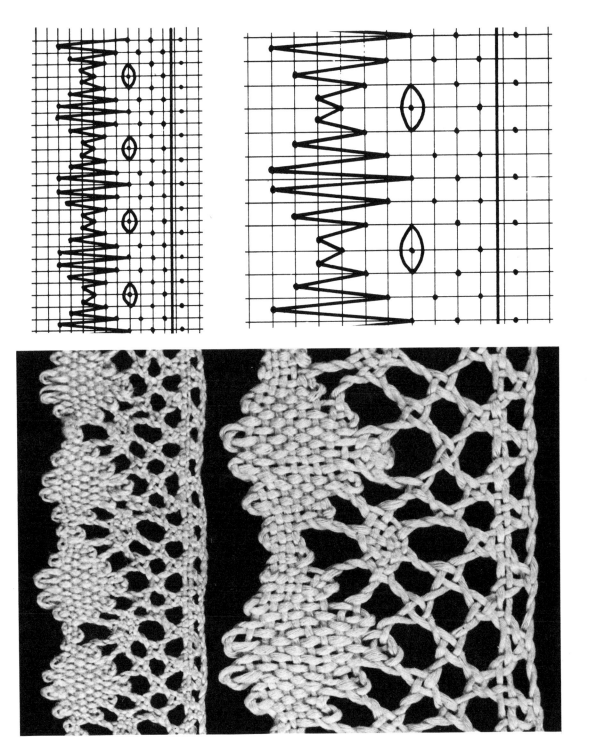

Figure 2. *(Top left) Drafting the pattern on graph paper helps you achieve uniform spacing of stitches. This draft is drawn on ⅛″/ 4mm graph paper, and the width of the pattern is 11 spaces, or 1⅜″/ 30mm. Stylized symbols and lines indicate the key parts of the lace, and dots show the location of pins.*

Figure 3. *(Top right) The same pattern as in Figure 2 drafted on ¼″/ 7mm graph paper. The width of the pattern is also 11 spaces but is 2¾″/ 70mm—exactly twice the width it was on ⅛″/4mm graph paper.*

Figure 4. *(Above) These two edgings were made using the patterns in Figures 2 and 3. The left lace, made with size 10/2 linen and rayon blend thread, was done using the ⅛″/4mm graph paper. The lace on the right, made from size 30/12 linen thread, was done using ¼″/ 7mm graph paper.*

Prickings. Traditionally, lace was not worked on drafted patterns directly. The patterns were taped to a stiff cardboard or parchment that fastened to a padded backing. A pricker, or a sharp pin, was used to pierce through all the places indicating the insertion of a pin (see Figure 5). Thus the structural skeleton of the pattern was transferred to the cardboard, or card. After removing the original drawing, the card—now called a pricking—was attached to the pillow and became the base on which the lace was made.

Although the pricking process is quite tedious and time consuming, it is used at times because it has many advantages. The pricked holes are in a rigid material that allows the pins to be inserted without bending and that holds them upright. Also, the stiff card will not be crumpled or pulled out of shape by the tension of the lace—thus the card can be reused.

Repeats. When making a lace pattern with regular repeats— sections of the pattern that duplicate themselves—it is best to make two or three pattern segments with several repeats each and leapfrog these as you progress. To do this, remove the pins from the beginning of your work when you reach the end of the pattern, roll up the finished lace, and transfer a segment of the pattern to the part of the pillow you are working on.

If the lace is going to be very long, make one pattern with several repeats to fit around your cylindrical pillow, even if you have to add extra padding under the pattern to make the repeats meet exactly. Periodically remove the beginning of the work to make a place for the newly completed lace. By doing this, you will be able to work the lace continuously around the pillow without shifting the pattern.

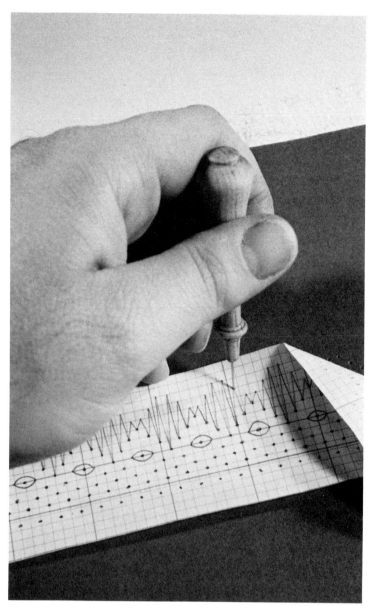

Figure 5. *A pin used to pierce the pattern to produce the pricking.*

WINDING BOBBINS

Once the pillow is dressed with an appropriate pattern, the next step is to wind your bobbins. If you do not have a bobbin winder (see Chapter 2, page 38), you have to do this by hand. To wind the bobbins manually, hold a bobbin in your right hand in an upright position with its head up. Using your left hand, start winding the thread at the bottom of the shank in a counterclockwise direction. Continue up and down the shank, making sure to wind the thread snugly and evenly. Do not overload the bobbin—too much thread will make the bobbin top-heavy and cause it to unwind unevenly.

When the shank is full, secure the loose end of the thread with a hitch. Do this by forming a loop on the end of the thread with your left hand so the end of the thread is hanging behind the portion of thread stretching from the bobbin to your left hand. With your right hand, push the head of the bobbin through the loop from the back, toward you (see Figure 6).

Tighten the hitch by holding the end of the thread in your left hand and turning the bobbin clockwise in your right hand. The hitch should either rest in a special groove (which some bobbins have) or just below the head of an ungrooved bobbin. If the thread is wound tightly on the shank, the hitch will stay on top rather than sink between the threads. If it does sink be-tween the threads, the hitch is likely to get tangled and make it very difficult to unwind the thread.

Some threads slip easily and need a double-looped hitch. For very slippery threads, such as silk ones, even a triple-looped hitch may be necessary (see Figure 6). The additional loops are added to the single hitch instead of repeating the single hitch two or three times. There is a distinct difference between two single hitches made one above another and a double-looped single hitch—although they both keep the thread from slipping, only the double-looped single hitch allows the thread to be wound and unwound without untying the hitch first.

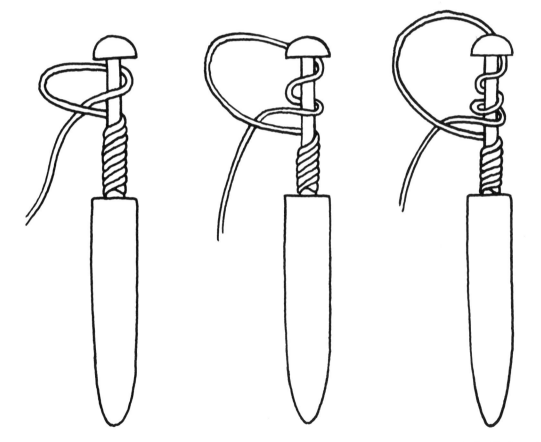

Figure 6. *How to hitch the thread after the bobbin is fully wound, from left to right: single hitch; double-looped hitch; and triple-looped hitch. The more slippery the thread, the more loops required on the hitch. Please note that in the double and triple-looped hitch, the single hitch is looped two or three times—you do not make two or three single hitches.*

To unwind the thread, hold the bobbin in an upright position in your right hand and turn it counterclockwise, pulling on the end of the thread with your left hand. The thread should unwind from the bobbin without disturbing the hitch. If you unwind too much, you can shorten the thread without undoing the hitch—with your left hand, pull on the loop between the hitch and the thread wound on the shank. With your right hand, turn the bobbin clockwise. This movement will wind the thread back on the shank. After the excess thread is rewound, tighten the hitch again.

You can wind bobbins separately and tie them together by an overhand knot (see Figure 7) to form a pair. Or you can wind two bobbins at the same time, one on each end of a piece of thread long enough to fill both of them.

You can simply loop the pair of bobbins wound on one thread over a pin stuck into the beginning of the pattern. If the pair is connected by an overhand knot, first push a pin through the knot and then stick it into the appropriate pinhole in the pattern. There should be about 3"/75mm of thread between the pins and the heads of the bobbins. Threads longer than this tend to tangle and make it harder to spot mistakes while you make the lace. In order to produce a lace of uniform quality, the tension of all the threads has to be kept the same—and all the bobbins should be carefully selected according to the thicknesses of thread used.

Attaching New Thread. If the bobbin runs out of thread in the middle of a piece of lace, wind the bobbin again with new thread and attach it to the lace using a square knot or a weaver's knot (see Figure 7). Because all knots are on the top face of the work, this side is considered to be the wrong side. Leave the ends of the knots uncut until the piece is finished—then cut them short. You will not notice them when the piece is turned to its right side.

THE CROSS AND TWIST

The technique of bobbin lace is very simple. With all the complex-looking designs of innumerable threads interwoven into fantastic images and a maze of different meshes, it is almost unbelievable that bobbin lace is based on only two different movements of bobbins—the cross and twist. Anybody learning bobbin lace *must* master these two basic motions.

To practice these movements, you will need two pairs of wound bobbins. Loop them over two pins placed close together in a horizontal line (see Figure 8). Each of your hands will manipulate one pair of bobbins. There are different ways of holding bobbins: some lacemakers keep their palms up while holding them; others do not hold their bobbins at all, but let them lie on the pillow and lift them over each other. Try these methods and others to determine which is best for you.

Now, hold the left pair, number 1, in your left hand and the right pair, number 2, in your right hand. To work the cross, pass the right bobbin of the first pair from your left hand over the left bobbin of the second pair to your right hand. At the same time, pass the left bobbin of the second pair to your left hand (see Figure 9). The twist is then worked by putting the right bobbin of each pair over the left bobbin of the same pair (see Figure 10).

No matter what combination these two basic motions are used in, they never change their direction. The cross is always left-over-right and the twist is always right-over-left. A cross and twist together form a half stitch. If the cross-twist sequence is repeated, the two pairs will interchange their places, and the formation is called a whole stitch (see Figure 11).

Figure 7. *Three knots used in bobbin lacemaking, clockwise from left: overhand knot, weaver's knot, and square knot. The overhand knot is used to tie wound bobbins together; the other two knots are used to tie a new length of thread onto a thread that breaks or runs out. The square knot is also used for tying off pairs of bobbins when you finish lace.*

When bobbins are hung on pins at the beginning of a pattern, they are always numbered by pairs 1,2,3, etc., from left to right. Whenever the pairs change their position, they are numbered by their new position in relation to the other pairs rather than by their original number. For example, after accomplishing the whole stitch (cross-twist, cross-twist) with two pairs of bobbins, the original pair, number 1, which is now in your right hand, will be referred to as number 2; and the pair that was originally number 2, now in your left hand, will be referred to as number 1.

It is very important that the bobbins are kept in order. Whenever you lay your work aside, make sure the bobbins are hanging straight down; and then secure them with a ribbon, an elastic, or a metal spring. If the bobbins do become tangled despite all precautions, before you can continue you must untangle them until all unwanted twists and crosses are straightened out and the work appears to have no mistakes in it.

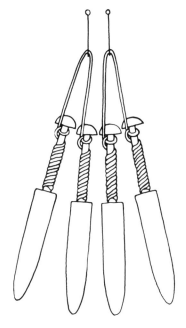

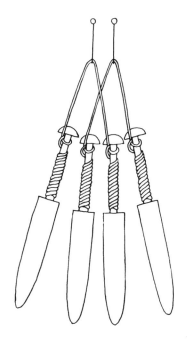

Figure 8. *(Left) Two pairs of bobbins are hung over the pins, the position they should be in before you begin making a cross.*

Figure 9. *(Right) The cross in the cross-twist sequence: the middle bobbins cross over each other, always left over right.*

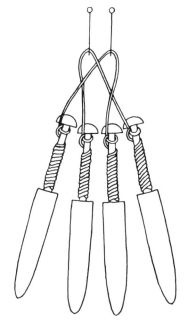

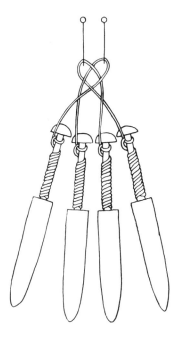

Figure 10. *(Left) The twist in the cross-twist sequence: after crossing the middle bobbins, the two pairs simultaneously twist from right to left, so the right threads twist over the left ones. The combination of cross-twist is called a half stitch.*

Figure 11. *(Right) By repeating the cross-twist sequence, a whole stitch is formed.*

BASIC STITCHES

To make bobbin lace, the two basic movements—cross and twist (described above)—are combined in stitches and grounds. Since the combinations are innumerable, I am going to discuss only the most basic and most frequently used stitches and grounds. Although the vocabulary of stitches included here may seem limited, you will be surprised how far you can go with knowing only these. And since all the stitches are based on the same principle, you will have no difficulty learning new combinations from other sources.

A good way to learn bobbin lace is to make the samples described below. After completing these samples, you will have a thorough understanding of how to follow the pattern on the drafts and how to handle bobbins. Since the projects in the following sections are composed of these stitches, the stitches make a good starting point. Copy the working drafts for each one, and either work over the drawing or make your-

Figure 12. *Several cross-twist sequences in succession form a braid.*

self a pricking from the draft to work on. The procedure for making each stitch is carefully explained and illustrated by both a drawing and a photograph of the completed sample.

Braid. A good stitch to begin with is the braid (see Figure 12), or plait, referred to in some lace books by the French word *bride*. To begin the braid you need two pairs of bobbins wound with 24″/610mm of thread on each bobbin. Place two pins in your pillow next to each other on a horizontal line, and hang the pairs of bobbins over the pins. There should be enough space between the pairs to allow the threads to lay comfortably next to each other. Begin doing the cross-twist sequence and repeat it until you run out of thread, spreading the bobbins after each of the sequences to push the stitches closer to each other and to keep the braid even and tight. By measuring the finished braid, you can gather some idea of how much thread must be wound on the bobbins initially to produce a desired length of braid.

Brussels Ground. The braid is very versatile and can be used in many combinations without adding any other elements. One of these combinations is the Brussels ground (see Figures 13 and 14). For this sample you need at least four pairs of bobbins each wound with 24″/ 610mm of thread. Pin them to the pillow the same way you did for the braid sample above. The number of cross-twist sequences in each braid must be the same. Although there is no rule as to how long the individual braids should be, the shorter they are, the stronger the lace will be.

After you finish the first row of braids, work the next row by letting pair 1 float, and braid pairs 2 and 3 together. Continue braiding together a pair from one braid with a pair from the next braid. This causes the rows of braids to alternate. Continue the cross-twist sequence until you finish this second row of braids, which will have the same number of cross-twist sequences as the first row. Then twist pair 1 several times and braid the first and second pairs together again to form the third row.

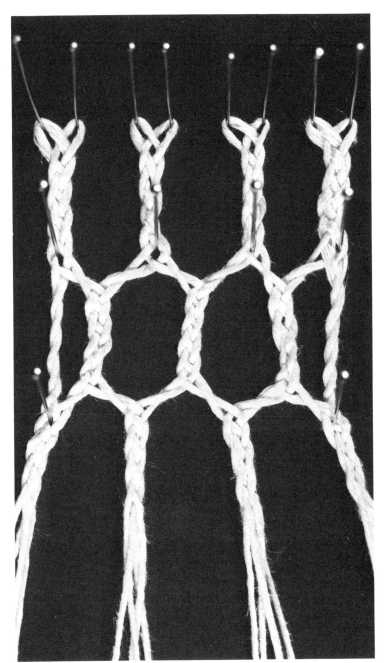

Figure 13. *(Above) This Brussels ground, made with six pairs of bobbins, illustrates how the pairs alternate from row to row.*

Figure 14. *In this sample of Brussels ground, the pins in the top row are evenly spaced. As the braiding progresses, notice how the pairs pull away from each other to form open spaces. The use of pins on the sides and at the bottom of the sample may be useful when you begin but are not ordinarily used.*

Intersecting Braids. Sometimes a design requires the intersecting of braids. One way to do this involves all four pairs of bobbins (see Figures 15 and 17). When the two braids reach the pinhole in the pattern indicating the intersection, handle each pair as if it were a single thread and make a half stitch. Insert a pin in the pinhole separating the pairs, and then make another half stitch so the pin is enclosed on all four sides. Now that the braids have intersected, continue braiding using each pair of bobbins as two threads again.

The second way to intersect braids is to use one pair of bobbins from each braid to make a whole stitch (see Figures 16 and 17). After you put the pin in the center of that stitch, braid those pairs—which have now taken each other's place—with the floating pairs waiting on either side.

The oldest bobbin laces were composed solely of braids—such narrow strips of lace are very easy to design (see Figure 18).

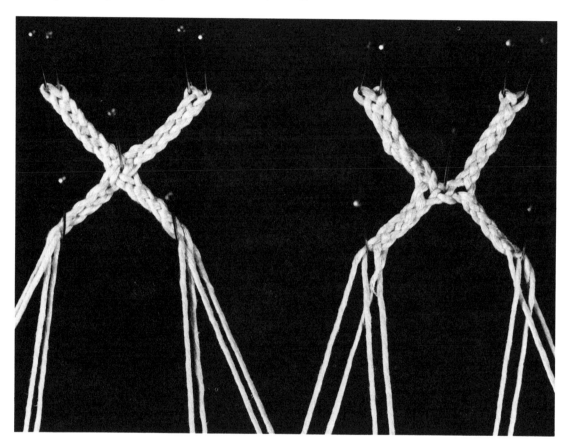

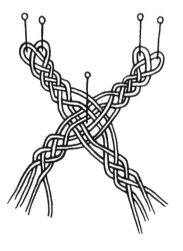

Figure 15. *(Left) Intersecting braids involving all four pairs of bobbins.*

Figure 16. *(Right) Another method of intersecting braids involving only pairs 2 and 3 in the cross.*

Figure 17. *(Above) Both methods of crossing the braids are strong and structurally satisfactory, although they differ in appearance. Left, intersecting braids using all four pairs of bobbins; right, intersecting braids using only pairs 2 and 3.*

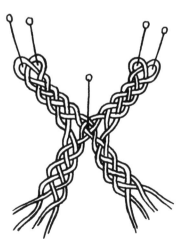

Square Leadwork. This very effective stitch, used in almost every type of bobbin lace, has many names—cutwork, tally, woven plait, seed stitch, and ear of wheat. Only two pairs of bobbins are needed. The basic procedure is that three of the four threads remain inactive while the fourth weaves around them. There are three basic shapes for this stitch—square, lozenge, and triangle.

The square variety (see Figures 19 and 22) starts with the two pairs of bobbins hanging from pins placed well apart. Twist each pair twice, do one cross, and then twist the right pair. Thus the right bobbin from the left pair travels over and under the threads of the right pair. This bobbin will now continue to weave over and under the remaining three passive bobbins to complete the square leadwork stitch. This is a deviation from the typical cross-twist sequence of all other stitches in lacemaking, as no other twist is made after the initial one by the right pair mentioned above. After that twist, you simply weave an active thread over and under three passive threads until a square is formed. Then complete the stitch by making a twist with each pair. As you do this, try to keep the three passive threads straight and spread apart to pack the woven thread up tightly so the threads are close together.

Lozenge Leadwork. To begin the lozenge-shaped leadwork (see Figures 20 and 22), place the two pins close together and make a whole stitch. Then weave the right thread from the left pair back and forth as you did to make the square leadwork. You can control the shape of the stitch by spreading the passive threads to widen the lozenge or by tightening the weaving thread to decrease the width. When the passive

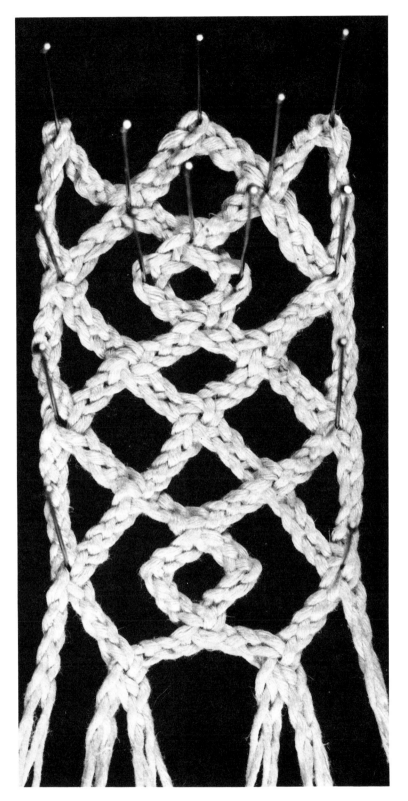

Figure 18. *A very simple composition of intersecting braids makes an effective piece of lace. This type of bobbin lace is among the oldest known.*

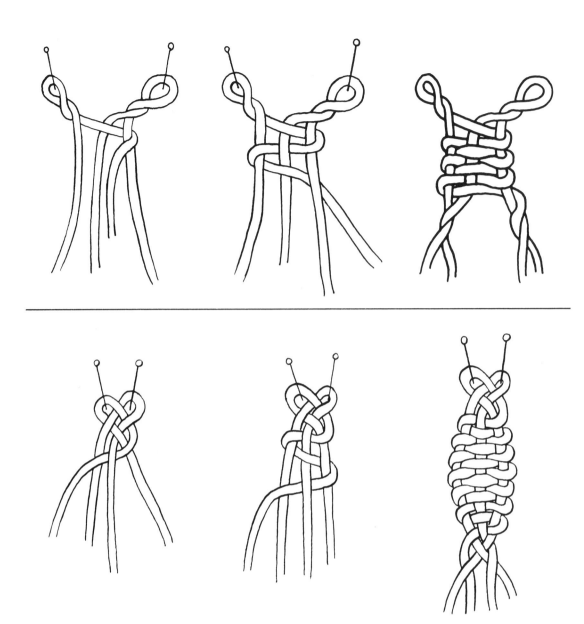

Figure 19. *(Top row) Making the square leadwork stitch: left, a cross followed by a double twist of the right pair; center, the left thread of the right pair, woven over and under the three remaining passive threads; right, a square formed and the stitch completed by making a twist with each pair.*

Figure 20. *(Center row) Making the lozenge leadwork stitch: left, begin with a whole stitch; center, weave the outside thread of pair 2 over and under the three remaining passive threads, widening the lozenge by holding the passive threads farther apart; right, the completed stitch, made by tightening the weaving thread to form the lower half of the lozenge, and then making a whole stitch.*

Figure 21. *(Right) The triangular leadwork, made by combining the top part of the square-shaped leadwork and the bottom part of the lozenge-shaped leadwork.*

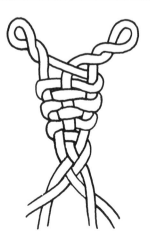

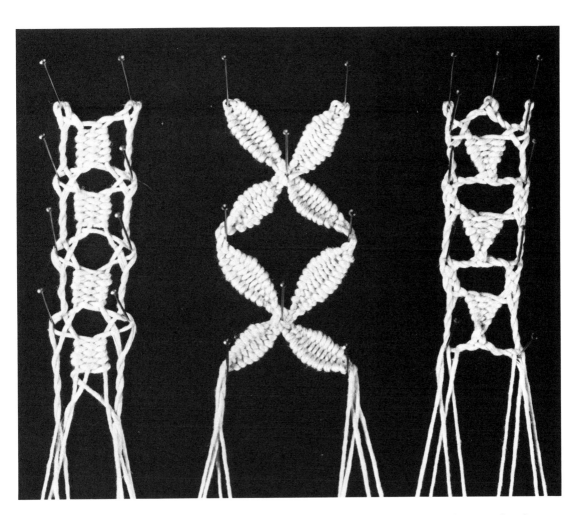

threads are fairly close together again, make a whole stitch to bring the shape to a point.

Triangular Leadwork. The triangular-shaped leadwork (see Figures 21 and 22) is a combination of both of the preceding shapes. It starts like the square, from two points set wide apart, and ends like the lozenge with a whole stitch.

Whole Stitch Ground. The whole stitch, linen stitch, and half stitch grounds are based on the action of a pair of bobbins, called a leader or worker, that acts as a weft and weaves through the rest of the threads, called passives. The worker weaves in a horizontal line through all of the passive pairs, connecting them together. The resulting lace is quite dense, and

for this reason these grounds are very often used for figures surrounded by airy net grounds.

As the name implies, the whole stitch ground is a network of whole stitches (see Figures 23, 24, and 25). To make it, place seven pins in the top row of pinholes in a pattern, and place one pin a little below the top row to the left. Hang a pair of bobbins over each of the pins, and make a whole stitch with the lower pair of bobbins (the leader, or worker) and the first pair on the left in the top row.

Next, let go of the pair that is now in your left hand, and transfer the pair in your right hand back to your left hand. Pick up pair 3 with your right hand, and do a cross-twist, cross-twist sequence with pairs 2 and 3. Repeat the same procedure until

Figure 22. *Three samples of narrow lace, from left to right: square leadwork, lozenge leadwork, and triangular leadwork. Some twists and braids were added to make a complete composition.*

you have used all pairs including—pair 8—the leader will have worked through all the threads in the top row and will be at the extreme right-hand side of the work. At this point, you should add another twist to the leader pair of bobbins, and put a pin in the appropriate pinhole, making sure the leader pair is above the pin. Holding this pair in your right hand, bring it around and under the pin. Then, with your left hand, pick up pair 7, make a whole stitch, and continue to work the leader pair through all the passive pairs

back to the left side. Although the leader pair is now going in the opposite direction, the movement of the crosses and the twists remains the same. The only difference between the second row and the first row is that after each whole stitch in the second row, the leader will end up in your left hand. After completing the second row, again place a pin in the appropriate pinhole and turn the leader around and under it. Repeat the first two rows several times until you can do the whole stitch ground quite easily.

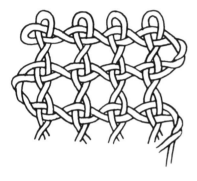

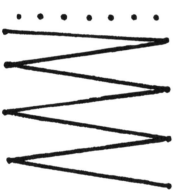

Figure 23. *(Top) In the whole stitch ground, one pair of bobbins slightly lower than the rest is chosen as a leader and is worked back and forth through the rest of the pairs.*

Figure 24. *(Above) Pattern for a whole stitch ground, which can also be used for linen stitch ground and half stitch ground. Since all of these grounds are based on the same principle of using one pair of bobbins as a leader, any one of these grounds could be substituted for another in the drafted pattern.*

Figure 25. *(Right) Whole stitch ground: the passive pairs of bobbins are at right angles to the leader pair.*

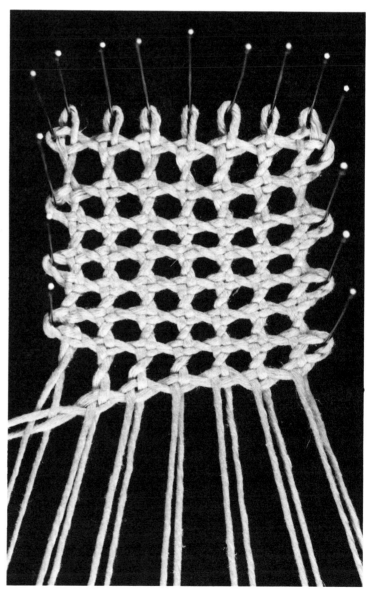

Straight Edge. There are times when a stronger or straight edge is needed on a piece of lace to allow, for example, the lace to be sewn to a fabric. In these instances, the leader pair in the whole stitch, linen stitch, or half stitch ground is not merely turned around and under a pin at the edge of the lace, but it exchanges roles with the last pair in the row to create a straight edge stitch (see Figures 26, 27, and 28).

Begin this sample the same way you began the whole stitch ground sample with eight pairs of bobbins. Hang the bobbins over the top row of pins, and, using pair 1 as the leader, proceed with whole stitches all the way across to the right edge of the sample. Notice that the pinholes at the edge of this sample are much closer to the body of the lace. After the last whole stitch in the first row, put the pin below both pairs 7 and 8 to the left of the last whole stitch.

Leaving the leader idle, take pair 7 in your right hand and pair 6 in your left hand, proceed toward the left using pair 7 as the leader. Do the same at the left edge. Then, after reaching the right-hand side again, engage the original leader in the last whole stitch and use it as a leader going back toward the left. Continue doing this for the entire sample to make the straight edges.

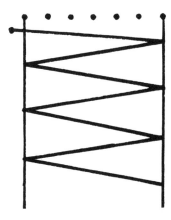

Figure 26. *(Top) Whole stitch ground with straight edges on both sides—these edges are quite strong.*

Figure 27. *(Above) Pattern for the whole stitch ground, linen stitch ground, and half stitch ground with straight edges on both sides.*

Figure 28. *(Left) Sample of the whole stitch ground. Notice how the straight edge decreases the width of the lace in comparison with the sample illustrated in Figure 25.*

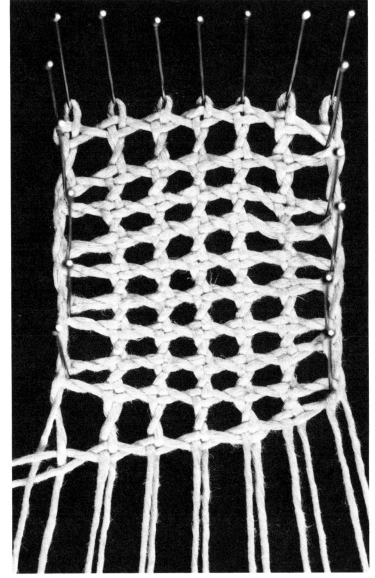

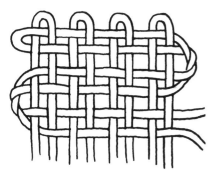

Linen Stitch Ground. The name of this stitch is very appropriate, since it resembles woven linen cloth (see Figures 29 and 30). Begin the sample the same way you began the whole stitch ground, with eight pins and bobbins. The only difference between working the linen stitch ground and the whole stitch ground is that the last twist in each of the stitches in the linen stitch ground is omitted. The procedure is:

cross-twist-cross the first and second pair; repeat with succeeding pairs until the leader works itself to the right side of the sample. Then, put in the pin, twist the leader twice, and turn it around and under the pin to start the second row.

Make another sample of linen stitch ground with a straight edge (see Figure 31). Remember to move the row of pinholes at the edges slightly closer to the center of the sample.

Figure 29. *(Above) Linen stitch ground, with its leader and passive pairs. Although the procedure of working this ground is similar to the one for the whole stitch ground, the result differs considerably.*

Figure 30. *(Right) Sample of the linen stitch ground. Since it is so dense, this ground is often used for working figures against a background of open meshes.*

Figure 31. *(Below) Linen stitch ground with two straight edges. It greatly resembles a woven fabric with selvages.*

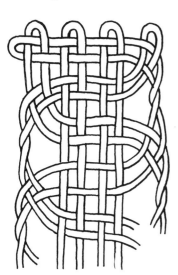

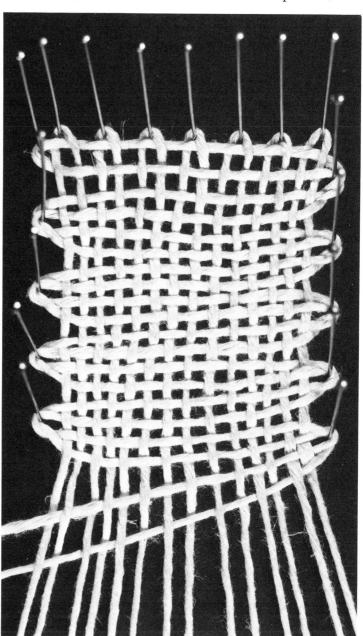

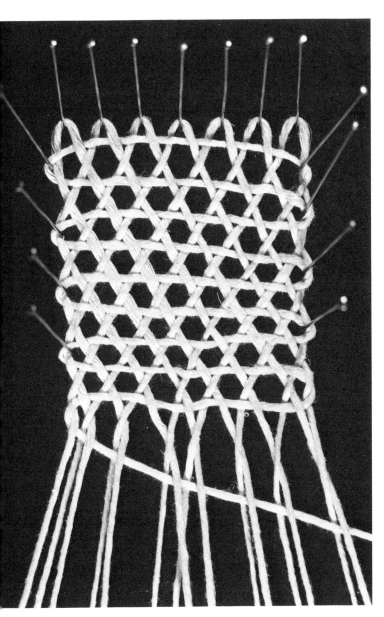

Half Stitch Ground.

This sample again requires eight pairs of bobbins (see Figures 32 and 33). Make a row of half stitches using pairs of bobbins in the following sequence: 1 and 2, 2 and 3, 3 and 4, 4 and 5, 5 and 6, 6 and 7, and 7 and 8. At this point, twist the leader twice and turn it around a pin. If you have done the row correctly, only one bobbin from the original pair 1 wove through to the right side, while the other bobbin is still part of the new pair 1.

Now make another row of half stitches with pairs 8 and 7, 7 and 6, etc., all the way to the left edge. Before you make each new half stitch, be sure both pairs of bobbins retain their previous twists (see Figures 32 and 33).

You can make the straight edge on the half stitch ground by doing a whole stitch with the leader and the last passive pair of each row, as in the whole stitch ground straight edge (see Figure 34).

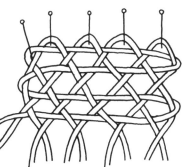

Figure 32. *(Left) The threads in the half stitch ground run diagonally to one another. Notice how only one thread of the leader pairs works itself from side to side horizontally.*

Figure 33. *(Above) Half stitch ground: the open spaces are hexagonal, and the overall appearance resembles chair caning.*

Figure 34. *(Right) By making a whole stitch with the leader and the edge pair and switching their roles, a very strong straight edge is formed on both sides of the sample.*

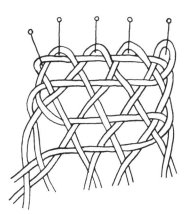

Torchon Ground. The torchon ground, maiden's net, and spider differ structurally from the previous three grounds in that there is no leader pair of bobbins—all pairs have equal importance. The torchon ground is the simplest and most basic ground of the three. Structurally, it is the whole stitch

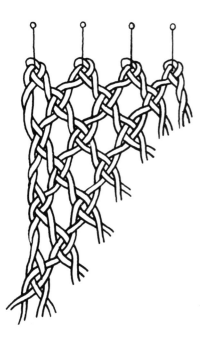

Figure 35. *(Top) Torchon ground, worked from top right to bottom left. Structurally this ground is the whole stitch ground worked on a diagonal.*

Figure 36. *(Above) Pattern for torchon ground: only the placement of pins need be drawn.*

Figure 37. *(Right) Sample of torchon ground.*

4 and 5, 3 and 4, 2 and 3, and 1 and 2.

Repeat these diagonal rows by going back to the next pair to the right in the top tow and working to the lower left with whole stitches. The sample will be completed when you make the last whole stitch with pairs 7 and 8 in the lower right-hand corner. Although these instructions are for working the sample from top right to lower left, you can also work from top left to lower right.

ground worked on a 45° angle (see Figures 35, 36, and 37).

To begin, hang eight pairs of bobbins over four pins placed in a horizontal line, two pairs to a pin. Make a half stitch at every pin, always using the two pairs hanging together on the one common pin. In the rest of the stitches that follow, place a pin in the middle of each stitch. Make a whole stitch with pairs 2 and 3 and then with pairs 1 and 2. Go back to the top row and make whole stitches with pairs

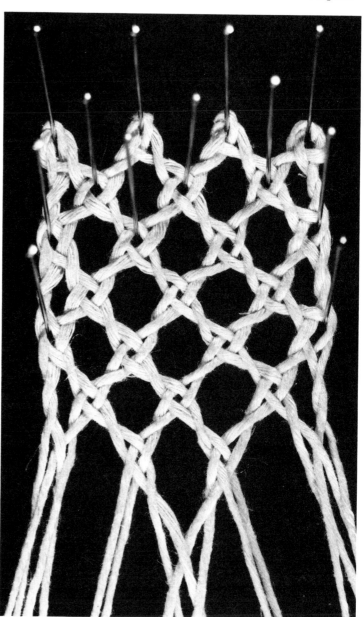

Maiden's Net. The twelve pairs of bobbins used for the sample of this ground is the minimum number you should ever use. The twelve pairs will cover an area large enough so you can easily see the repeat of the maiden's net. See Figures 38, 39, and 40 for illustrations of this ground.

Hang twelve pairs of bobbins over the top row of six pins, two pairs to each pin. Make a half stitch with all the pairs, always using the two pairs hanging together on one common pin. With pairs 2 and 3 make a whole stitch and place a pin in the middle. Do the same with subsequent pairs in the following sequence: 1 and 2, 3 and 4, and 2 and 3. This completes the diamond shape formed by the four whole stitches.

Move to the next diamond on the right, and repeat the same procedure working with pairs 5, 6, 7, and 8. After completing this second diamond, make one half stitch with pairs 3 and 4 and another with pairs 5 and 6. The pairs 3, 4, 5, and 6 will be used for making the next diamond shape below and between the first two diamonds. When you finish this diamond, make a whole stitch with pairs 1 and 2 and a half stitch with pairs 3 and 4. Now you are ready for the next diamond to be made with pairs 1, 2, 3, and 4. After completing it, go back to the top row and construct a diamond with pairs 9, 10, 11, and 12. Complete the sample by working the diamonds in diagonal lines from top right to lower left.

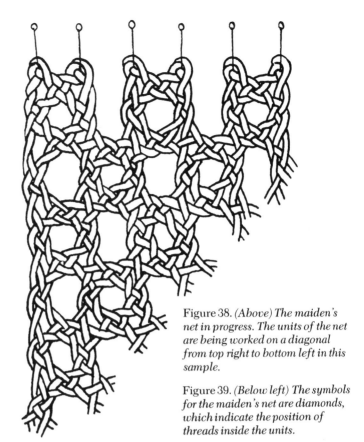

Figure 38. *(Above) The maiden's net in progress. The units of the net are being worked on a diagonal from top right to bottom left in this sample.*

Figure 39. *(Below left) The symbols for the maiden's net are diamonds, which indicate the position of threads inside the units.*

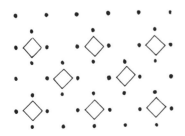

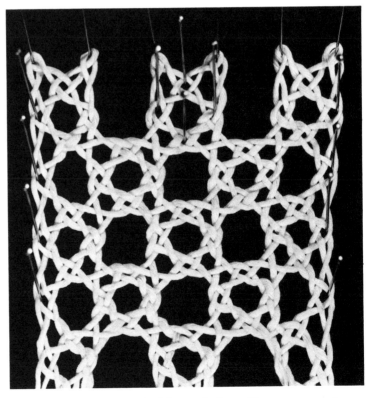

Figure 40. *Completed sample of the maiden's net. The empty spaces in a checkerboard pattern separate the dense motifs.*

Spiders. Although in this sample spiders form the entire ground, they are very effective as a single element combined with a simple ground. The spider sample (see Figures 41, 42, and 43), just like the maiden's net sample, requires twelve pairs of bobbins hung two to a pin.

To start, make a half stitch with each of the two pairs sharing a single pin. Make an additional twist with pairs 1 and 12. Work a horizontal row of whole stitches with pairs 2 and 3, 4 and 5, 6 and 7, 8 and 9, and 10 and 11, always laying the pairs down before you pick up the next two. Next, make one whole stitch with pairs 1 and 2 and another with pairs 5 and 6. Now begin the actual spider by forming a linen stitch with pairs 3 and 4. Continue making linen stitches with pairs 2 and 3, 3 and 4, 4 and 5, 3 and 4, 2 and 3, 4 and 5, and 3 and 4. Make one twist on pairs 2, 3, 4, and 5 to form the lower legs of the spider.

Go back to the top row and make one whole stitch with pairs 7 and 8 and another with pairs 11 and 12. Pairs 8 through 11 are now ready for the second spider, which is worked the same way as the first one. After the completion of the second spider, make whole stitches with pairs 6 and 7, 5 and 6, and 4 and 5. Add one twist to pair 1 and work whole stitches with the following pairs in this order: 1 and 2, 2 and 3, and 3 and 4. Give pair 1 an additional twist and continue working whole stitches with pairs 1 and 2 and then 2 and 3. After adding one more twist to pair 1, make a whole stitch with pairs 1 and 2.

Continue working the spider motifs in diagonal lines from top right to lower left, separating the individual spiders by rows of whole stitches until the entire sample is finished.

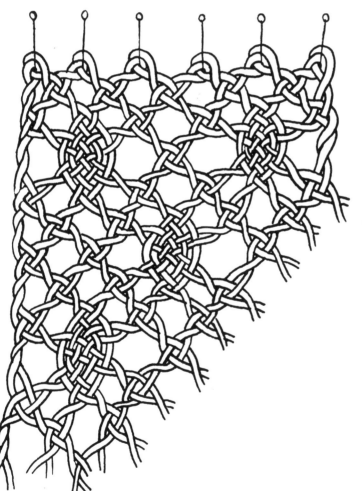

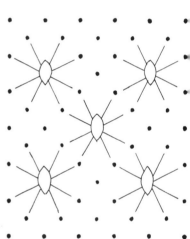

Figure 41. *(Left) In this drawing four of the five spiders have been completed.*

Figure 42. *(Above) The symbols for spiders are surrounded by pinholes, which indicate where there will be torchon ground.*

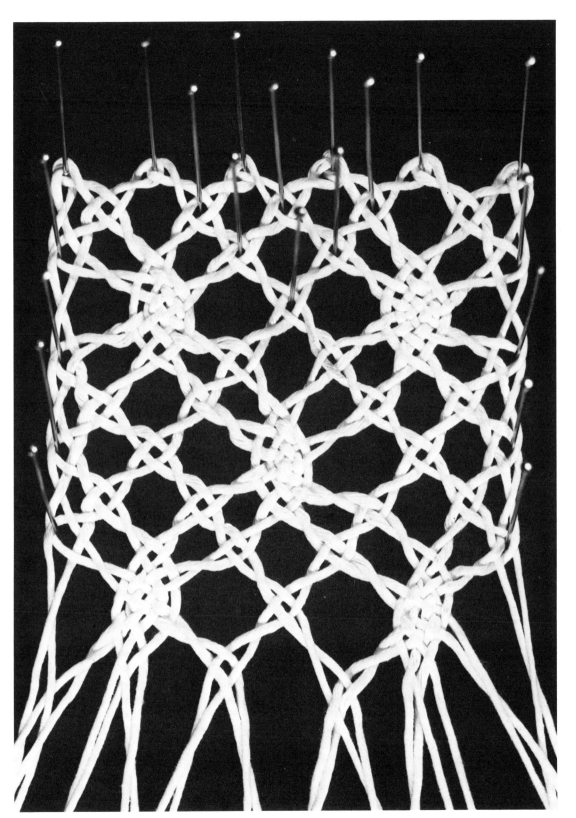

Figure 43. *Five spiders framed by lines of torchon ground form the finished sample. Torchon ground could be substituted for some of the spiders to break the regularity.*

STRAIGHT LACE

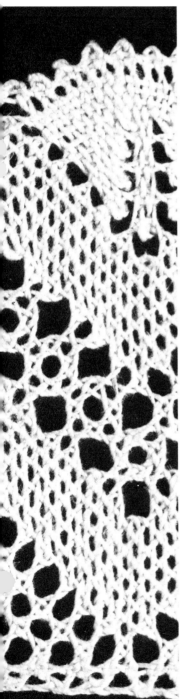

Straight lace is the most common type of lace, although its use varies considerably from country to country and region to region. What distinguishes straight lace from all other types is the fact that the same threads are used to form both the ground and the figures simultaneously in one piece. In most cases, the same number of threads that begin the piece end the piece, although threads may be added and deleted according to the design and shape of the particular lace.

This technique does not limit itself to narrow edgings—laces several feet wide have been made using hundreds of bobbins. The lace made by this technique can incorporate a vast variety of stitches used in unlimited combinations. Because straight laces are basically compositions of several stitches, the purpose of this section is to explain how to combine these stitches.

In the directions for the projects in both this section and the one on tape lace that follows, I will describe only the details of how to combine the stitches already learned to avoid repetition of basic stitch construction. Of course, although the projects in this section will sufficiently teach the basic principles of bobbin lace, they are by no

means all that can be done in straight lace. When you complete these samples, you will be able to use the basic principles to experiment, explore, and create your own individual laces.

The first samples of the straight lace below are the braided laces, followed by several exercises in torchon lace. The rest of the samples are so distinct in their use of color and stitches, that although they are based on torchon lace principles, they are more properly classified as peasant laces.

BRAIDED LACE

The simplest straight laces are those composed of braids and leadwork. And the most suitable leadwork to combine with braids is the lozenge leadwork, because it begins and ends in a point. Patterns for the braided laces contain very few pinholes, and a pricking would be insufficient. You must work from a draft complete with symbols pinned to the pillow and work the lace directly over it. In the drafts prepared for the following samples, the leadwork is symbolized by the outline of its shape; braids are represented by thick lines; and threads of single pairs are pictured by thin lines.

Sample One. The first sample (see Figures 1 and 2) is worked with twelve pairs of bobbins. Begin by hanging pairs 1, 2, 3, and 4 over one pin in the upper left-hand corner, and pairs 9, 10, 11, and 12 over one pin in the upper right-hand corner. Pairs 5 and 6, and 7 and 8 are added after the two top corner lozenges have been formed with pairs 3 and 4, and 9 and 10 (see Figure 3). Make braids with all the pairs—when you reach the intersections of the braids, make them according to the method described on page 50. Complete the sample by working the remaining braids and lozenges.

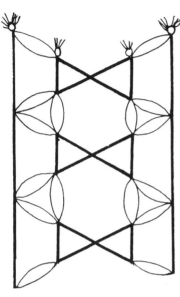

Figure 1. *(Above) Since patterns for braided laces contain only a few pinholes, which are insufficient information, the lace is worked directly over the draft. This draft— for the first sample—contains thick lines indicating braids and thin outlines indicating lozenge lead- works. The little circles at the top of the draft represent knots, and the little lines attached to these circles indicate how many threads were knotted together.*

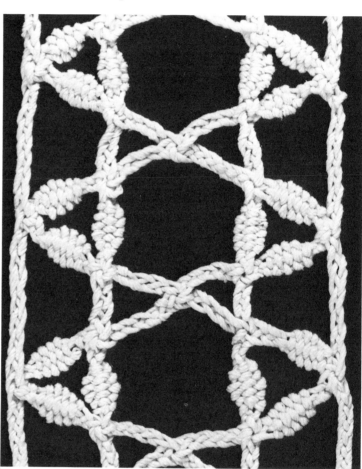

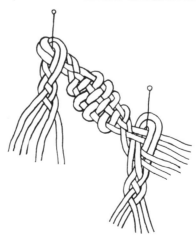

Figure 2. *Sample One—braided laces are thick and strong, giving them a sound structure. Because of this quality, they are very effec- tively combined with other stitiches.*

Figure 3. *(Left) Pairs 5 and 6 are added after the first lozenge lead- work is completed at the upper left- hand corner with pairs 3 and 4. The same thing is done at the upper right-hand corner.*

Sample Two. This sample is similar to the first one except for the addition of a flower motif (see Figures 4 and 5). Again, twelve pairs of bobbins are pinned to the pillow at the places indicated on the pattern. This time, though, pairs 3 and 4 and pairs 9 and 10 form braids instead of leadwork. Except for this difference, the first half of the repeat is worked in the same manner as in Sample One above. The flower motif consists of four lozenge-shaped leadworks followed by three rows of Brussels ground and another four lozenges.

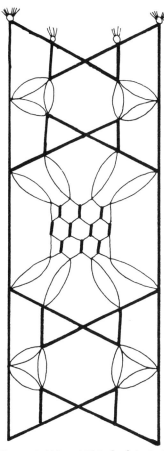

Figure 4. *(Above) This draft is similar to the first, except that a flower motif has been added. The thin lines in this flower motif represent single pairs of bobbins.*

Figure 5. *(Right) Sample Two— braided laces can be designed with large openings because of their inherent structural strength.*

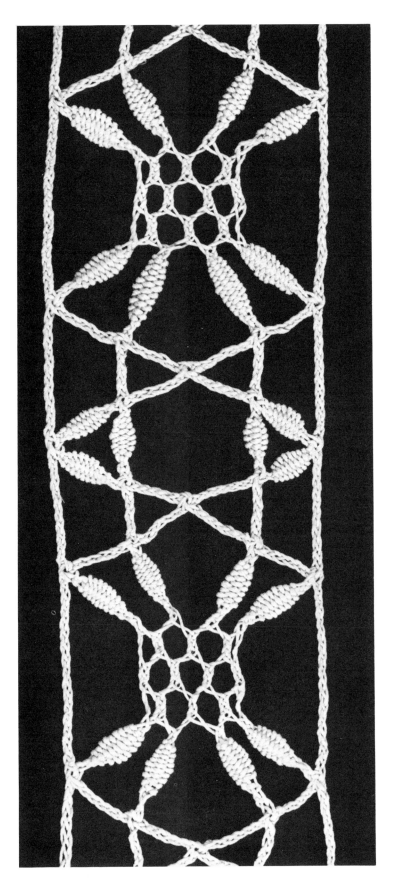

Sample Three. Although this sample contains the same flower motif as Sample Two, it differs considerably from both Samples One and Two. Both edges, as well as the spaces between the flowers, are made in whole stitch ground (see Figures 6 and 7). Fourteen pairs of bobbins are all hung on the top row of pins as indicated in the pattern. Notice that pairs 1 and 14 are both leaders throughout the entire work, and that they work symmetrically from opposite sides. Pairs 2 and 3, and 12 and 13 are passive pairs. Pairs 4 through 11 are alternately involved in the whole stitch ground and in the formation of the flower motif.

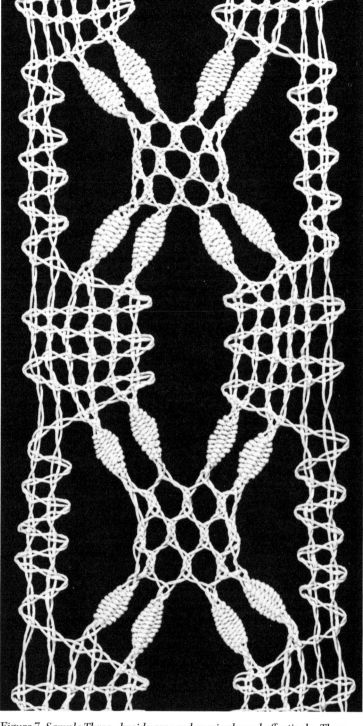

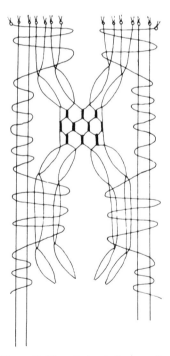

Figure 6. *The whole stitch ground in this third sample is worked symmetrically beginning with leader pairs in the upper right and left corners.*

Figure 7. *Sample Three—braids are used sparingly and effectively. They are combined both with lozenges and whole stitch ground along the two edges and between the flower motifs.*

TORCHON LACE

Torchon lace is the simplest of the grounded laces, which are an important type of straight lace. Grounded laces are, basically, those laces in which figures are connected by grounds or nets rather than by the bars of braided laces.

Torchon lace is unique among these grounded laces for two reasons. All other grounds are worked on angles from 50° to 70°, whereas torchon lace grounds are worked on a 45° angle. Torchon ground bears its name because it is the most commonly used ground in torchon lace, and it is characterized by its geometrical shapes and straight lines. Fans and spiders so often used in torchon lace are two of the few examples of curved lines appearing in torchon lace.

In Figures 8, 9, and 10, torchon ground is combined with the linen stitch ground in a diamond shape. This will help you become familiar with the working of the foot edge reinforcement pair and the transition from torchon ground to the linen stitch and vice versa. Hang fourteen pairs of bobbins over the top row of seven pins, two pairs on one pin, as if you were starting the torchon ground sample in the previous chapter.

Work the torchon ground on the diagonal, leaving pairs 7 and 8, 6 and 9, 5 and 10, and 4 and 11 to to be picked up for the diamond. The foot edge is worked just like the straight edge of the torchon ground, except that pair 2 reinforces the edge here at the same time that pair 3 forms the straight edge with pair 1 after intersecting with pair 2 (see Figure 11).

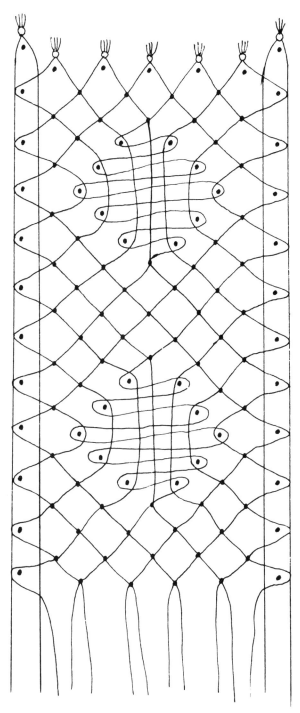

Figure 8. *Draft for the torchon ground combined with linen stitch ground in the form of diamonds.*

After completing the torchon ground along the top half of the diamond, work the whole diamond in the linen stitch. To start, form a linen stitch with pairs 7 and 8, and continue back and forth (from left to right) adding a pair at each side and forming a loop edge with the leader pair. After you add pairs 4 and 11, leave out the pairs one by one at each turn of the leader, until the last linen stitch is formed by the pairs 7 and 8 (see Figure 12). Observe that the original pair 8 is the pair that became the leader—after forming the diamond, it becomes pair 7.

When you complete the diamond, work the torchon ground along its bottom half and continue until that ground outlines the top of the next diamond.

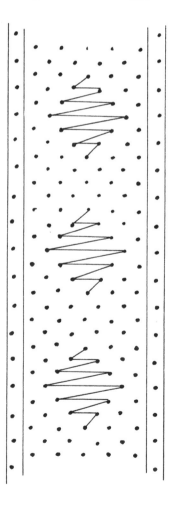

Figure 9. *(Left) The pattern for this sample indicates that both edges are reinforced.*

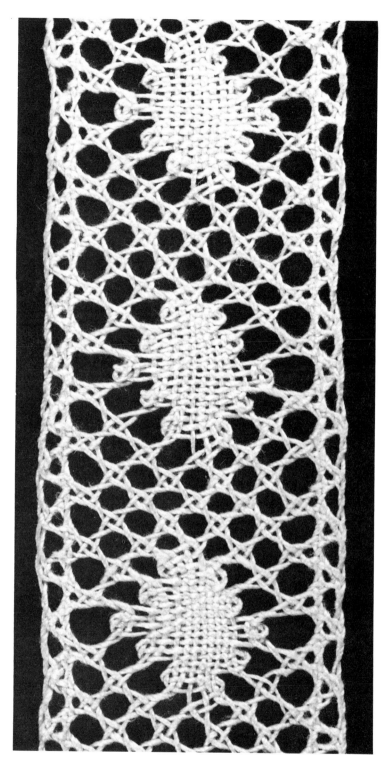

Figure 10. *(Above) Sample of torchon ground and diamond-shaped linen stitch ground. The reinforced edge is strong and neat, while the linen stitch ground figures stand out against the airy torchon ground field because of their density.*

Figure 11. *(Right) Foot edge reinforcement. Pair 2 forms the reinforcement edge while pair 3—after intersecting with pairs 2 and 1— forms the outside edge.*

Figure 12. *(Below) The leader pair 8 weaves back and forth, picking up an additional pair at each side until it weaves through pairs 4 and 11. This is the widest part of the diamond. The leader forms the lower half of the diamond in the opposite manner, dropping one passive pair at each turn.*

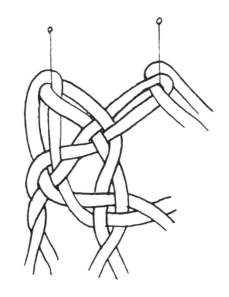

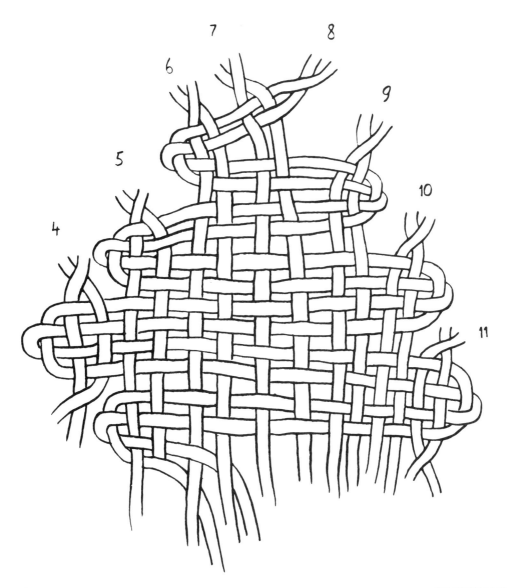

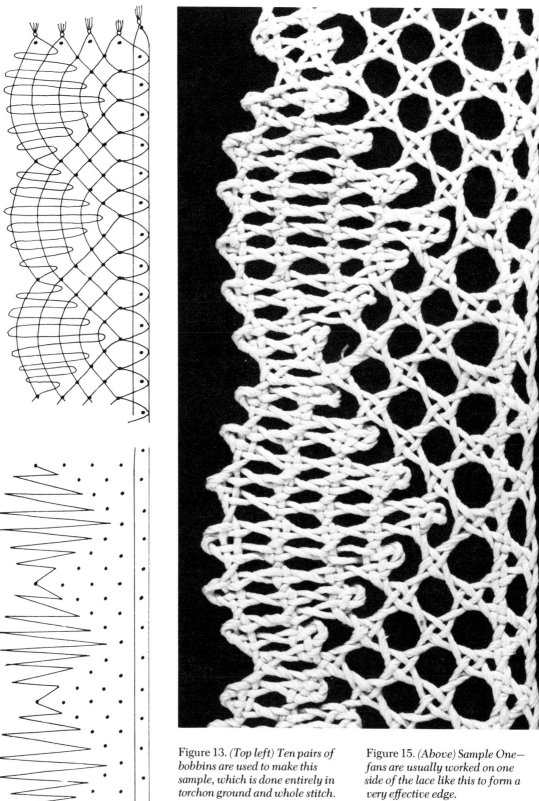

Figure 13. *(Top left) Ten pairs of bobbins are used to make this sample, which is done entirely in torchon ground and whole stitch.*

Figure 14. *(Left) The zigzag lines on this pattern indicate the path pair 2 takes to construct the fan.*

Figure 15. *(Above) Sample One— fans are usually worked on one side of the lace like this to form a very effective edge.*

THE FAN

Fans are scalloped forms that are used on the edges of torchon lace. Most of the time they are worked on one edge only, but there is no reason why they cannot be worked on both edges. When a fan is done on only one edge of the lace, this edge is called the head of the lace. The straight edge is called the foot of the lace. The work done between the foot and the head is called the body of the lace.

Whether you work the foot of the lace on the right or left side is a matter of personal preference. For the sake of consistency, all laces done in this chapter are worked with the foot on the right side. If you wish to work the samples with the foot on the left side, simply draft the pattern in reverse.

There are many ways to work fans, and in this section I introduce five of the more common types. For simplicity, the body and the foot of the first four samples below are worked identically. This does not mean, in any way, that you are limited to these stitches. You can combine the fan with a wide variety of grounds, a few of which are used in the last sample.

Sample One. This sample (see Figures 13, 14, and 15) uses ten pairs of bobbins hung over the top horizontal row of pins, two pairs over one pin. To begin, work the torchon ground starting from the upper right-hand corner and moving on a diagonal, engaging all the pairs except 1, 2, and 3. Then proceed with the fan, working entirely in the whole stitch. Pair 2 becomes the leader and works toward the left through pair 3; then it turns around a pin and goes back through both the same pair and pair 1. Each time the leader reaches the right side, it picks up another pair of bobbins until it picks up pair 6. Then the leader continues making the rows of whole stitches, but it drops a pair each time it reaches the right side (see Figure 16).

When the leader meets with pair 1 in the last row, the two pairs form a whole stitch and exchange roles. The original leader becomes the passive pair 1, and the original pair 1 becomes the leader. At this point, you should work the torchon ground until you reach the top outline of the second fan.

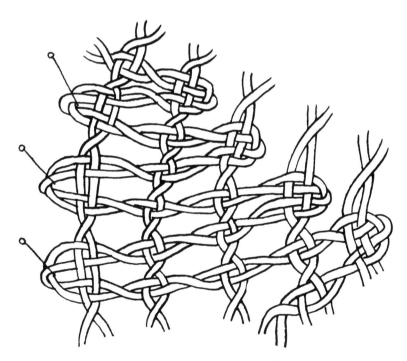

Figure 16. *While constructing the first half of the fan, the leader picks up an additional pair each time it reaches the right side. The lower half of the fan, constructed by dropping one pair each time the leader reaches the right, is a mirror image of the first half.*

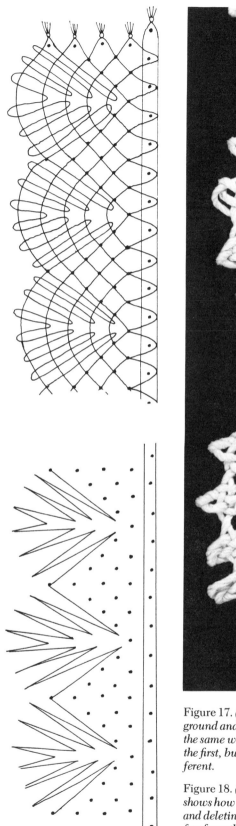

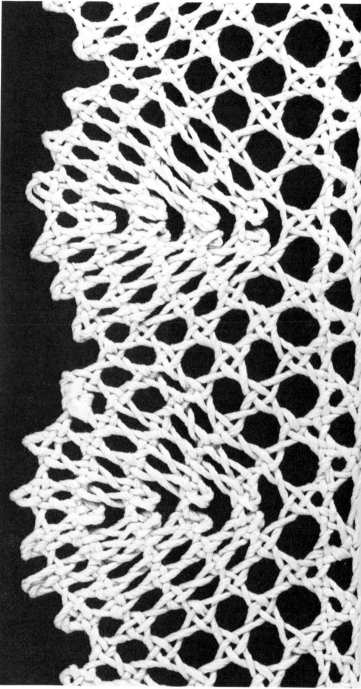

Figure 17. *(Top left) The torchon ground and foot edge are worked the same way in this sample as in the first, but the fan is slightly different.*

Figure 18. *(Left) The zigzag line shows how the sequence of adding and deleting pairs by the leader differs from the first sample (see Figure 14).*

Figure 19. *(Above) Sample Two— the difference in the appearance of this fan and the previous one (see Figure 15) is subtle but nevertheless distinctive.*

Sample Two. The torchon ground and the foot edge in this sample are worked the same as in the previous sample. The fans are worked in the whole stitch again, but the sequence of adding and deleting the pairs involved in the fan differs (see Figures 17, 18, and 19).

Pair 2 acts as leader first and works through pairs 3, 4, 5, and 6 and back through all of them including pair 1. Then, rows become one pair shorter until the leader works through pairs 1 and 2 only. At this point, the leader should start to add one more pair in each row, and the last row of the fan should include pair 6 (see Figure 20). When the leader works back to the left edge, it forms a whole stitch with pair 1 and exchanges roles.

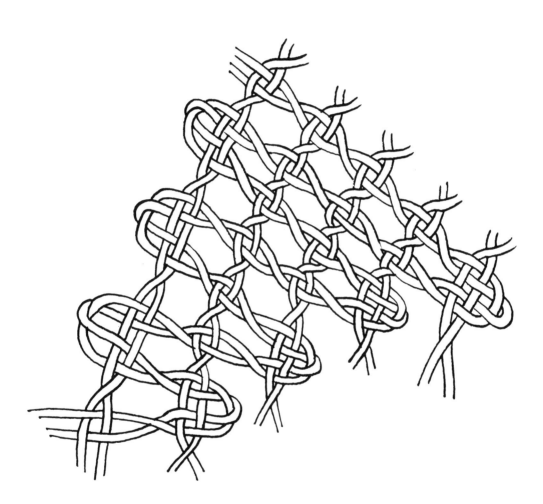

Figure 20. *When the first half of the fan is worked, the leader drops the passive pairs one by one in succession, while in the second half of the fan, the leader adds one passive pair at each turn.*

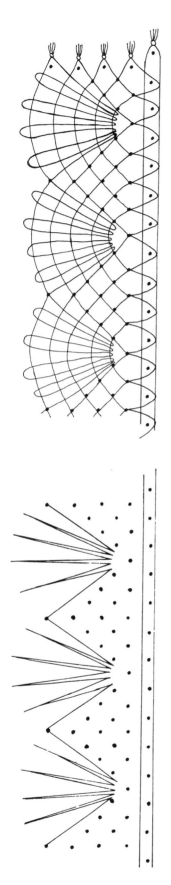

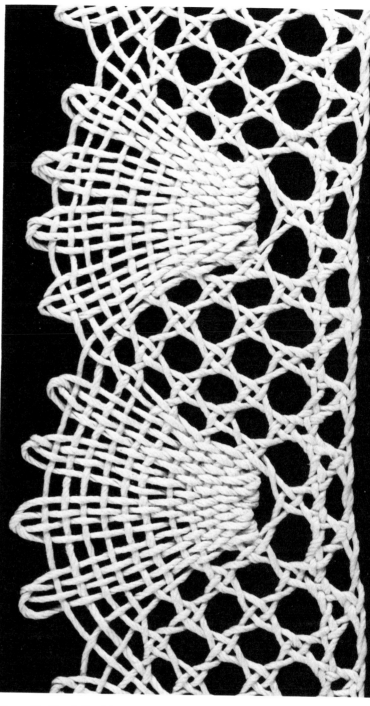

Figure 21. *(Top left) Although the fan is worked differently in this sample, the torchon ground and foot edge are worked in the same manner as they were in the first two samples.*

Figure 22. *(Left) The pattern shows that no passive pairs are added or deleted by the leader in the construction of the fan.*

Figure 23. *(Above) Sample Three— this type of fan is very dense at its vertex and open and airy along its edge.*

Sample Three. This fan is done in linen stitch, and the leader works through all five passive pairs of bobbins in all ten rows. The shape of the fan results from packing the threads of the leader closely together at the one side of the form and spreading them loosely at the edge (see Figures 21, 22, 23, and 24).

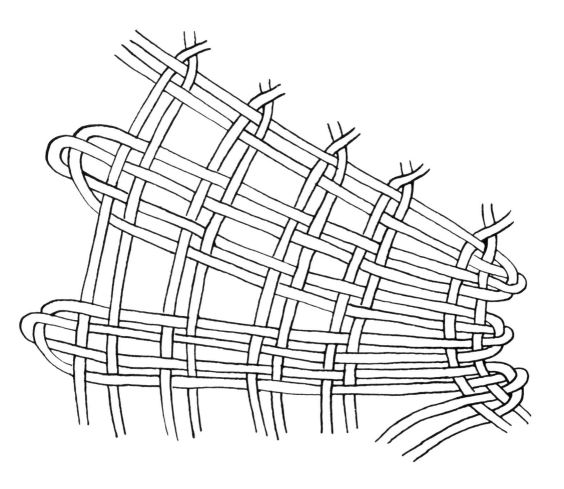

Figure 24. *The effective appearance of this fan depends upon equal spacing of the threads of the leader as it passes back and forth through the passive pairs.*

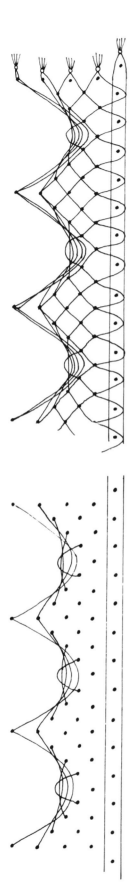

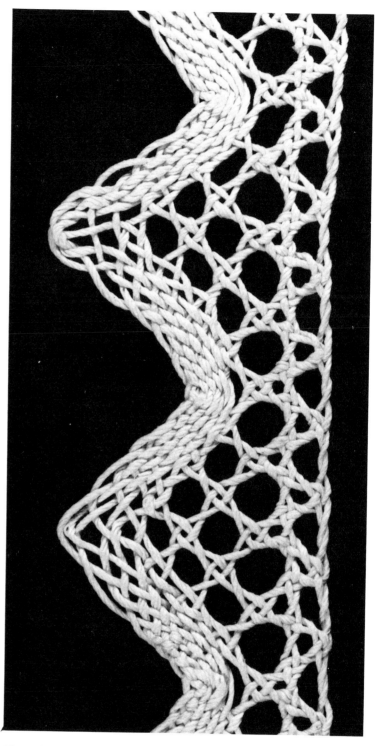

Figure 25. *(Top left) This fourth type of fan also has scalloped edges, but it has open spaces where the fans would normally be.*

Figure 26. *(Left) The lines in this pattern show the paths of the pairs of bobbins that form the scallop.*

Figure 27. *(Above) Sample Four— an entirely different feeling is created by working the scallops in this kind of fan.*

Sample Four. Although this fan forms scalloped edges like the previous three, it differs from the other samples in that it creates open spaces where the other fans were located. The foot and ground are worked identically to the previous three samples, leaving pairs 1, 2, and 3 to form the scallop in linen stitch (see Figures 25, 26, and 27).

There are two ways to treat pairs 2 through 6 before using them with pair 1 in the linen stitch. Before you begin the scallop, either twist pairs 2 and 3—as 4, 5, and 6 already are twisted—or untwist 4, 5, and 6. Then, using pair 1 as the leader, make a linen stitch with pairs 2 through 6. After pair 1 makes the last linen stitch with pair 6, the original pairs 2 through 5 become leaders one by one and make linen stitches through the original pair 6. At this point all the pairs have changed positions—the original pair 1 is now pair 6, and the original pair 6 is pair 1 (see Figure 28).

Repeat the same procedure so the new pair 1 becomes the leader and makes linen stitches through pair 6. Pairs 2 through 5 in turn become leaders and do the same thing. After the last two pairs make a linen stitch, put a pin in place—you will be ready to work the second scallop as soon as you complete the torchon ground between the first and second scallops.

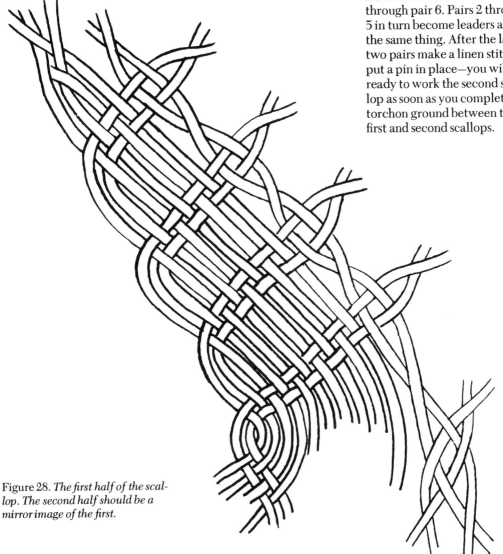

Figure 28. *The first half of the scallop. The second half should be a mirror image of the first.*

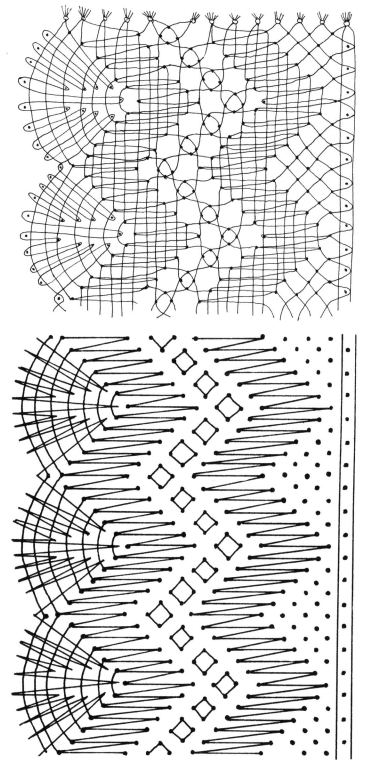

Sample Five. In this sample, torchon ground, half stitch, maiden's net, and linen stitch are worked with thirty pairs of bobbins (see Figures 29, 30, and 31). The transition from the torchon ground to the half stitch ground is exactly the same as the transition from the torchon ground to the linen stitch diamond (see page 67–69).

Following the draft from the very beginning, make the torchon ground section first, followed by the half stitch ground strip. The transition from the half stitch ground to the maiden's net is slightly different. After pairs 9 through 12 form the first motif, pairs 11 and 12 form a half stitch and pairs 13 and 14—which were left from the half stitch ground—form another half stitch. Pairs 11 through 14 form a third maiden's net motif, and pairs 13 through 16 form the fourth motif. Always remember to form the half stitch before making the motif. If you forget, the figure formed will look more like a section of torchon ground than a maiden's net.

After all four maiden's net motifs are finished, continue making the second half stitch ground strip, always taking in one more pair from the right before each turn of the leader and leaving one pair out at the left side after each turn of the leader. Before taking in any of the pairs from the maiden's net motifs, make sure you worked a half stitch with them first. After finishing the half stitch ground up to its first change of direction, there should be eight pairs of bobbins ready for the fan.

The fan is worked as follows. Pair 1 becomes the leader—it always intersects with pair 2 in a whole stitch and with all of the rest of the pairs in the linen stitch. Pair 1 works first from left to right through the next six pairs and then back to the left.

Figure 29. *(Top) Draft for the fifth sample fan.*

Figure 30. *(Above) The sample is worked from right to left, beginning with the torchon ground followed by the half stitch ground strip, maiden's net, another half stitch ground strip, and finally the fans.*

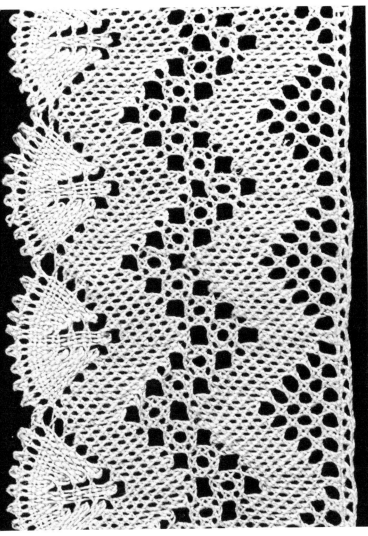

After forming a loop edge, it works through only five pairs. And so it goes for two more times, the leader always taking in one less pair. Next, the leader goes through seven pairs straight through the center (see Figure 32). Be sure to twist pairs 5, 6, 7, and 8 before the leader works through them to separate this line from the upper half of the fan.

After the leader works itself back to the left edge of the fan, pairs 5, 6, 7, and 8 again twist to separate this line from the lower half of the fan. The lower half of the fan is then worked the same way as the upper half, but in reverse.

When you finish the fan, all of the pairs are ready to be taken one by one into the half stitch ground followed by the maiden's net motifs, the half stitch ground, and the full triangular field of torchon ground, which prepares the way for repeating the whole process.

Figure 31. *Sample Five—see how effective the fan can be when combined with other stitches.*

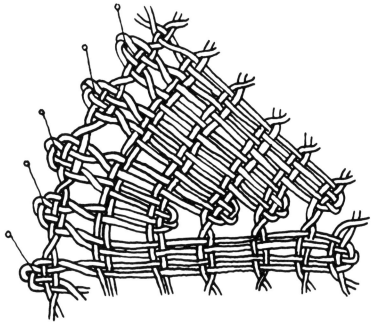

Figure 32. *The fan in this sample is very similar to the fan in Figure 19, except that the leader runs the full length of the fan in the center.*

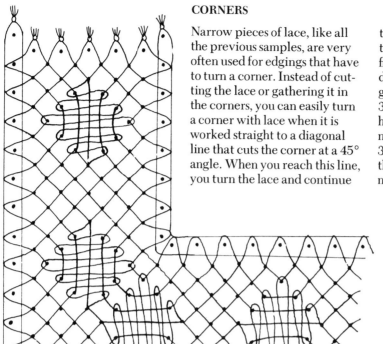

CORNERS

Narrow pieces of lace, like all the previous samples, are very often used for edgings that have to turn a corner. Instead of cutting the lace or gathering it in the corners, you can easily turn a corner with lace when it is worked straight to a diagonal line that cuts the corner at a 45° angle. When you reach this line, you turn the lace and continue to make it in a mirror image of the first half of the corner. The first sample of a corner is the diamond motif in torchon ground (see Figures 33, 34, and 35), while the second illustrates how a fan is treated when a corner is reached (see Figures 36, 37, and 38). I described both of these samples—without the corner—earlier in this section.

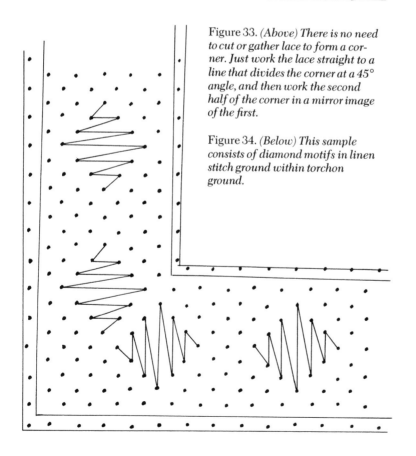

Figure 33. *(Above) There is no need to cut or gather lace to form a corner. Just work the lace straight to a line that divides the corner at a 45° angle, and then work the second half of the corner in a mirror image of the first.*

Figure 34. *(Below) This sample consists of diamond motifs in linen stitch ground within torchon ground.*

Figure 35. *Corners are very often used in household linens—when they are constructed in one piece, they are not only attractive but also much more durable than corners that are cut or gathered.*

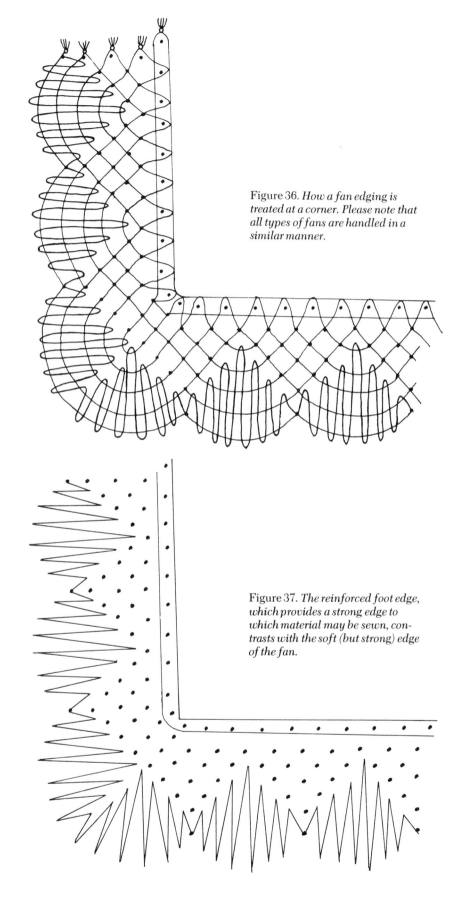

Figure 36. *How a fan edging is treated at a corner. Please note that all types of fans are handled in a similar manner.*

Figure 37. *The reinforced foot edge, which provides a strong edge to which material may be sewn, contrasts with the soft (but strong) edge of the fan.*

Figure 38. A fan worked around a corner in this way produces a soft, rounded corner that is less likely to roll or fold as a straight, sharp corner would tend to do.

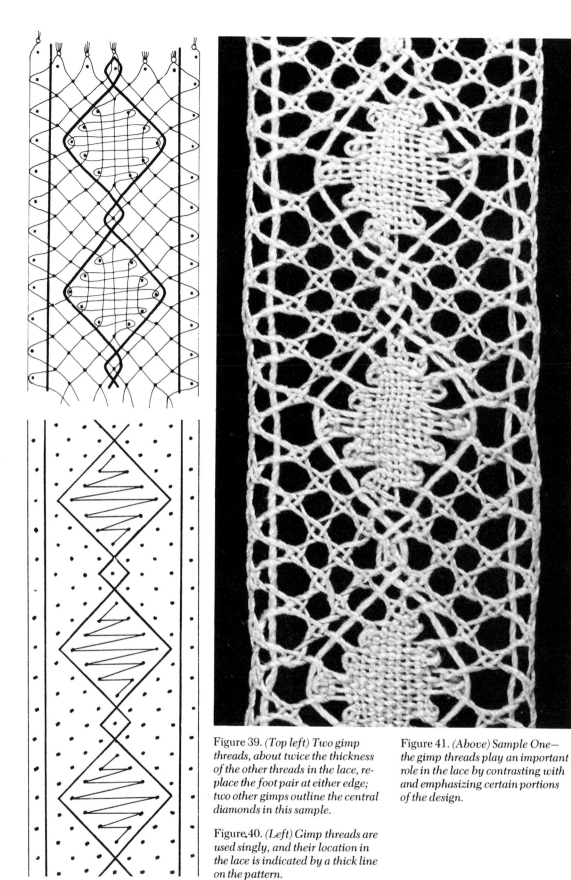

Figure 39. *(Top left) Two gimp threads, about twice the thickness of the other threads in the lace, replace the foot pair at either edge; two other gimps outline the central diamonds in this sample.*

Figure 40. *(Left) Gimp threads are used singly, and their location in the lace is indicated by a thick line on the pattern.*

Figure 41. *(Above) Sample One— the gimp threads play an important role in the lace by contrasting with and emphasizing certain portions of the design.*

ADDITION OF A GIMP

A gimp, sometimes spelled "guimp," is a single thread much thicker than the rest of the threads used on the same piece of lace. The gimp thread is used singly rather than in pairs, as is usually the case, and it should be at least double the thickness of the rest of the threads. This thread is often used for outlining figures and thus emphasizes their difference from the background.

Sample One. To illustrate how a gimp is used in lace, the diamond shape within the torchon ground sample is worked here with the addition of a gimp. Altogether there are four gimps— one at each edge replacing the foot pair, and two gimp threads outlining the diamonds (see Figures 39, 40, and 41).

The gimp must be enclosed by two threads of a pair every time it intersects with any pair (see Figure 42). For example, when you work the left foot edge of the sample, pair 2 twists; the gimp is passed through as if it were the right bobbin of another pair, and pair 2 is twisted again. Then pair 2 goes on to form the foot edge with pair 1. Enclosing the gimp thread with the pair of threads, and locking it in place by the two twists, controls the exact direction of the gimp. Whether the gimp is used at the edge or anywhere else within the lace, it is always worked in the same way.

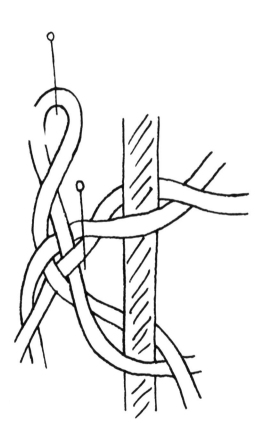

Figure 42. *You must enclose the gimp thread within two threads of a pair each time it intersects with any pair to secure it in the lace.*

Sample Two. This example, using seventeen pairs of bobbins and three gimp threads, is a little more elaborate (see Figures 43, 44, and 45)—it illustrates how a gimp is treated when it doubles back within the same stitch. The design consists of a zigzag row of linen stitch diamonds surrounded by triangular fields of torchon ground. On the right side, the triangular shape of the torchon ground is outlined by two single gimp threads, which cross over each other.

On the left side of the diamonds, there is a single gimp which moves in a zigzag motion. This gimp is of particular interest, since it repeatedly intersects two pairs of bobbins in the torchon ground and doubles back toward the left again within the same stitch (see Figure 46). You do this by placing the gimp between twisted threads of two subsequent pairs. Then you insert a pin—although there is no pinhole indicated on the pattern—for the gimp thread to turn around. Next, you twist the last pair of bobbins through which the gimp was led, and weave the gimp back through the same pair. At this point you twist that pair again to enclose both strands of the gimp. Do not twist the following pair, but pull the gimp through the same intersection of threads that it was previously woven through when it was going in the opposite direction.

If the gimp weaves back and forth within one stitch through more than two pairs of bobbins, only the last pair will have three twists in it at the turning point to hold the gimp in place. The rest of the pairs will surround both threads of the gimp within one opening by a twist from each side.

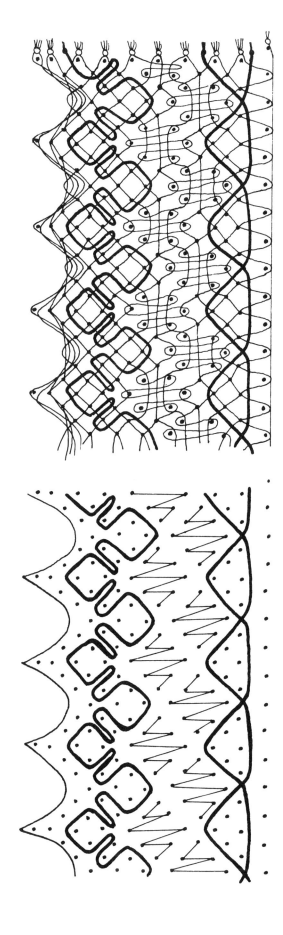

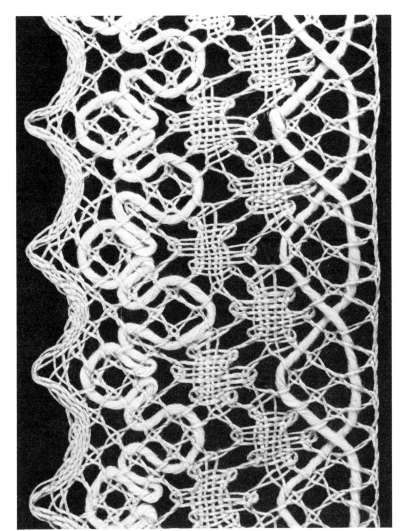

Figure 43. *(Top left) This more elaborate sample incorporates several stitches, including torchon ground, linen stitch diamonds, and scalloped fans, as well as three gimps.*

Figure 44. *(Bottom left) The zigzagging gimp adjacent to the scalloped edge repeatedly intersects with the torchon ground. The diamond shapes formed by this gimp alternate with the linen stitch diamonds.*

Figure 45. *(Right) Sample Two— the richness and visual impact of lace that combines several stitches and gimp threads is clearly evident in this sample.*

Figure 46. *The gimp threads are enclosed within the twists of the pairs they pass through. At the points where the gimp returns within the same stitch, it is locked in place in the manner shown here.*

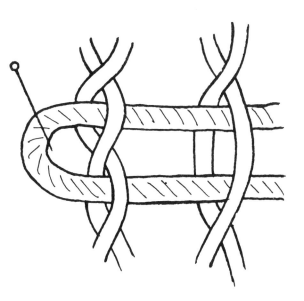

THE GIMP AS A DESIGN ELEMENT

In some cases the gimp can be a very dominant part of the design, and it sometimes forms the only design element in lace piece. This often occurs in Russian peasant laces, where the curves and zigzag movement of the gimp form a strong linear design and surround a figure made in a different stitch—usually the linen stitch. This figure is placed most often in a torchon background.

Since the example of the gimp as the main design element here (see Figures 47 and 48) is done entirely in torchon ground and since the gimp is worked in the fashion already described above in the two previous examples, no further explanation is required. Please note that the working drawing is not necessary, because the pricking with the line indicating the direction of the gimp is self-explanatory. The piece it-

self is a table runner with all figures defined by the single gimp thread. The gimp used in the central figures was wound on two bobbins as a pair and worked simultaneously on both sides of each figure to avoid a knot on the gimp. At the extreme point of the figure where the two gimps meet again, they are knotted together. After the whole piece is finished, the knot is trimmed short.

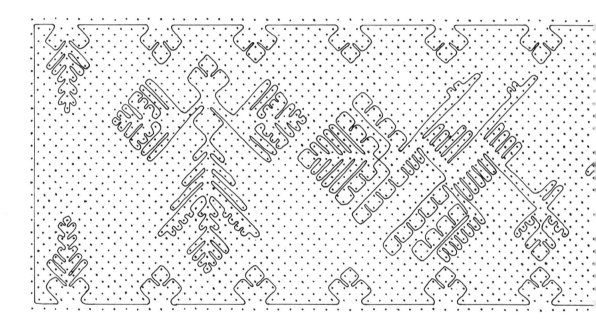

Figure 47. *Pattern for the table runner project.*

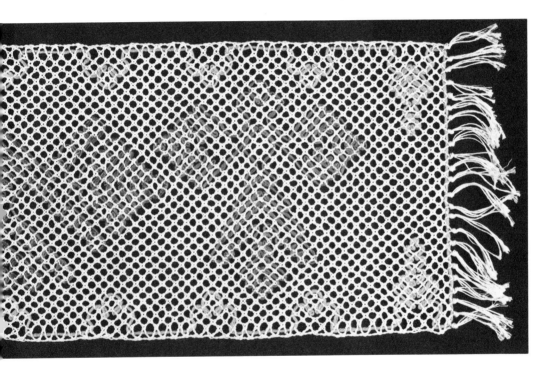

Figure 48. *The gimp becomes a quite effective, independent design element by virtue of its color, thickness, and multi-directional movement.*

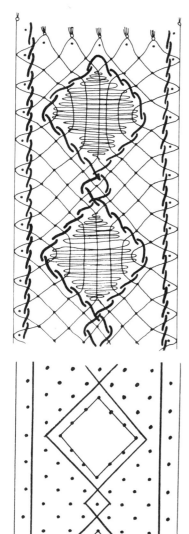

Twined Gimp. Twined gimp is very rarely used in Western Europe, but it is a favorite in Russia and Eastern Europe. The twined gimp consists of a full pair of bobbins wound with thread as thick as or slightly thicker than the rest of the threads. Very often the gimp is of a different color than the rest of the lace.

When you use gimp threads, you must twist or twine them over each other toward either the left or the right; but you must twist or twine them consistently in one direction to give a raised cordlike effect. The gimp pair always twists just before a whole pair of bobbins is laid in between the gimp threads. The thread of gimp that goes over the whole pair of bobbins will go under them the

Figure 49. (Top) The twined gimp in this sample replaces the foot edge reinforcement pairs and outlines the leadwork diamonds.

Figure 50. (Above) The twined gimp is represented, as usual, by a single thick line on this pattern

Figure 51. (Right) Note the distinctive cordlike appearance of twined gimp. It was used very often in old Russian and eastern European laces.

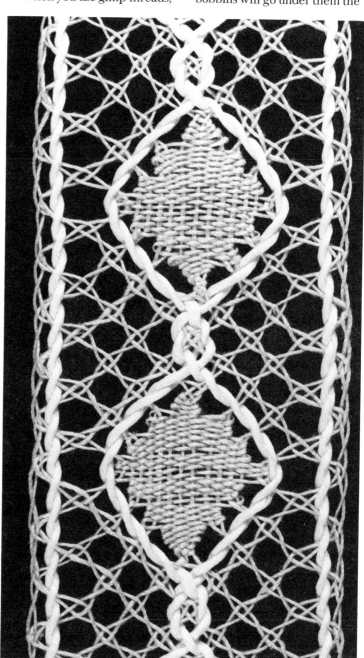

next time. Since the gimp twists around the pairs but does not intersect with them, the gimp threads take up a very narrow space in the lace, a space even narrower than that taken up by a regular passive pair. In the example here of the diamond in torchon ground plus a twined gimp, the gimp replaces the foot edge reinforcement pairs and outlines the diamonds (see Figures 49, 50, and 51), just like the single gimp did. All four of the gimp pairs twist toward the left in this sample. The pairs of bobbins laid through the gimp threads twist in the usual way (see Figure 52).

The diamond outlined by twined gimp in this sample is not in linen stitch as the previous samples using the same pattern were (see Figure 40), but is woven into a multi-paired leadwork (see Figure 53). Traditionally, whenever twined gimp was used in straight lace, it always outlined shapes worked in this type of leadwork.

The diamond shape starts with pairs 7 and 8 forming a whole stitch. The left thread of pair 8 becomes the weaver, weaving back and forth through the three remaining threads. When the weaver reaches pairs 6 and 9, it weaves around them also. (Please note that all the added threads are passive.) After the weaver adds pairs 5, 10, 4, and 11, the leadwork achieves its maximum width. If the leadwork pulls in when you first try this, catch the turns of the weaver by pins, especially every time you add a new pair.

Next, weave the bottom half of the diamond, periodically dropping pairs 4 and 11, then 5 and 10, and lastly 6 and 9. After the weaver weaves over and under the remaining three threads of pairs 7 and 8, all four threads form a whole stitch. The result is a definite diamond shape with slightly jagged edges.

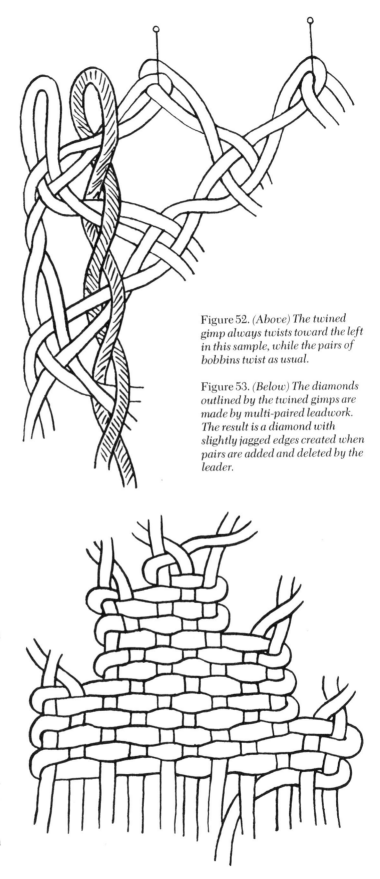

Figure 52. (Above) The twined gimp always twists toward the left in this sample, while the pairs of bobbins twist as usual.

Figure 53. (Below) The diamonds outlined by the twined gimps are made by multi-paired leadwork. The result is a diamond with slightly jagged edges created when pairs are added and deleted by the leader.

COLORED THREAD

In Russian and Eastern European peasant lace, color plays a very important role. As a part of very colorful costumes, lace reflected the colors used in the woven patterns and embroidery on costumes. The basic red, blue, and yellow have always been favorites; but some unusual combinations of pink, mint green, peacock, and brown colors are found, especially in silk laces.

Since lace edgings and insertions were used on everyday clothes and household linens, their durability and sturdiness were of more importance than the airiness and fragility of the Western European laces. Thus many of the examples in this section may seem solid and dense. Also, the use of color precludes very elaborate combinations of stitches that could cause difficulties in figuring out where to lead certain threads in order to achieve the intended color effect.

The best example of simple, definitive, and striking color effect is the use of a colored gimp thread that is thicker than the rest of the threads used in the lace. Figure 54, for example, has a red gimp thread, and, even in such a simple example, the whole mood of the lace changes (compare this figure to Figure 40). The table runner in Figure 48 is also a striking example of the impact of color in gimp—the torchon ground is in natural linen, while golden, brown and red gimps add the color accent.

Figure 54. *This sample uses the same pattern illustrated in Figure 40. The bright red gimp used here makes all the difference and changes the mood of the entire lace.*

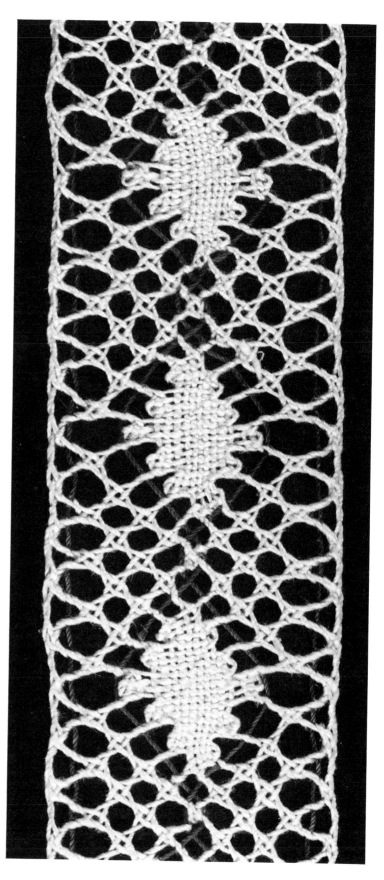

Color Accent. Gimp is by no means the only way color can be incorporated in lace. You can use colored threads to single out an unusual path of a pair of bobbins—such a path becomes more obvious and dominant in the design when the thread is in color. One example is the narrow golden edging where the golden leader is replaced by a blue passive pair 5 at regular intervals (see Figures 55, 56, and 57). If this blue pair were also golden, only the openings formed each time the regular leader was replaced would be of any design importance. But since the pair is a blue, the path of scallops can be followed more clearly than the openings themselves. To help relate this thread to the rest of the lace, pair 7 (which forms a straight line) is the same blue.

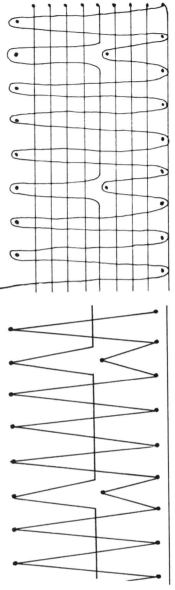

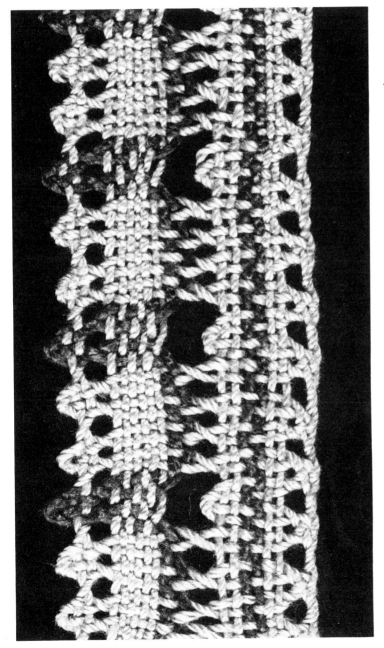

Figure 55. *(Top) Draft for a narrow edging. Pairs 5 and 7 are blue, while the rest are golden. By changing the color of two pairs, the path of those threads is accentuated.*

Figure 56. *(Above) The path of pair 5 is shown on the pattern because it assumes the role of a leader; pair 7, although it is also blue, is not marked because it is a passive pair.*

Figure 57. *(Left) This is a very simple example of how to use color in lace. To get a more complicated design, you could use a number of colors in one lace or a number of pairs next to each other of the same color to produce a strip of color.*

A much stronger pattern effect is achieved in the next narrow strip (see Figures 58, 59, and 60) where pairs 5 and 8 weave a whole stitch regularly through pairs 6 and 7. When pairs 5 and 8 meet each other in the center, they intersect in a whole stitch and thus work themselves to their original position. This movement forms a lozenge-shaped pattern that is further emphasized by the loops of the two regular leaders, which do not go all the way to the center between lozenges and thus do not intersect each other in a whole stitch there as they do three times within the lozenges.

The threads of pairs 5 and 8 are orange and are slightly thicker than the rest of the threads, which are white. Also, pairs 3 and 10 are of the same orange thread to help introduce color to the borders.

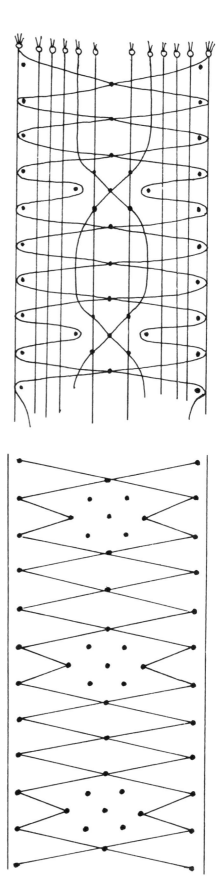

Figure 58. *(Top right) The color orange in pairs 5 and 8 and pairs 3 and 10 is used in this sample to emphasize the directional movement of some of the pairs.*

Figure 59. *(Bottom right) The color of the threads is not indicated on patterns, nor are the paths of the colored threads if they are passive, as they are here.*

Figure 60. *(Opposite page) A lovely edging. To relate the borders to the colored, central portion of the lace, colored thread is also used in pairs 3 and 10.*

Alternating Color Dominance. In the following two examples, the colored threads assume different functions—they become dominant and obvious at certain portions of the piece, while they become almost invisible in between these portions. This creates the illusion that the colored threads are discontinued, i.e., used in certain areas and then cut off. Instead, the colored threads are concealed, ingeniously, and this prevents the necessity of cutting them off and tying them back on.

In the first sample of red and blue fans, the basic threads forming the arches of the fans, the torchon ground, and some of the wide linen stitch border are a natural color (see Figures 61, 62, and 63). The first fan is worked in linen stitch with blue pair 1 as a leader. The leader works back and forth three times through red pair 2 (original pair 5) and natural color pairs 3, 4, 5, and 6.

The fourth time the blue leader works in linen stitch through the fan, it goes all the way to the right through all the pairs. At the extreme right it makes a loop edge, and, forming the blue stem of the fan, it works back to the left. The second half of the fan is completed as a mirror image of the first half. After working the torchon ground and the adjoining linen stitch border, the next fan is made using the red-colored pair as the leader. The blue pair, which worked the first fan, is now pair 2 and forms the outer left arch of the red fan. Thus the red and blue threads alternate in forming fans without becoming too conspicuous in between.

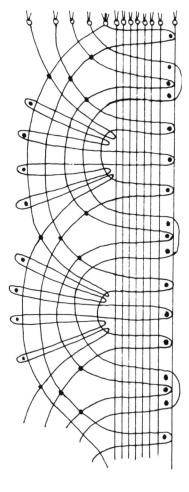

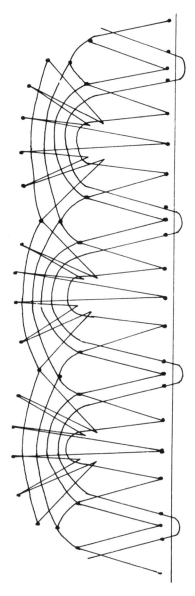

Figure 61. *(Right) Draft for fans that alternate in color. In this sample, pair 1 is blue and pair 5 is red; thus the first fan is blue, the second red, and so on.*

Figure 62. *(Far right) From this pattern you can see that the alternating colors in the fans result from allowing each colored pair to be the leader in one fan and passive in the next, when the second color becomes the leader.*

Figure 63. *(Opposite page) Three of the passive pairs in this sample are in color to visually connect both halves of the edging.*

Although the next sample is not any more difficult to make, it seems more complicated, since there are more colors involved (see Figures 64, 65, and 66). Eighteen pairs of bobbins are used in this piece, and the color sequence is, from the left: two natural pairs, two orange, three natural, one pair consisting of one orange and one red thread, two natural pairs, one pair consisting of one orange and one green thread, three natural pairs, two orange, and two natural.

The threads are disguised here in the leadwork squares. You just choose which one of the several colors available for each square will dominate by weaving through the three remaining threads. The three passive threads of the leadwork squares are thus completely covered, and their continuity is visually interrupted. When following a regular pattern, such as the one in this sample, keep track of all the colors. In this edging, for example, you should

make sure that when the central orange leadwork square is woven, no natural color threads are used. And be sure to switch the red and green threads from left to right or vice versa before weaving them into the orange leadwork if they are to appear on the opposite side after the square is completed (see Figure 67).

The only time all of the colored threads are visibly led through the lace is in the lozenge-shaped section between the clusters of leadwork squares.

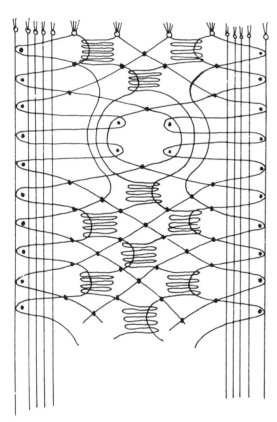

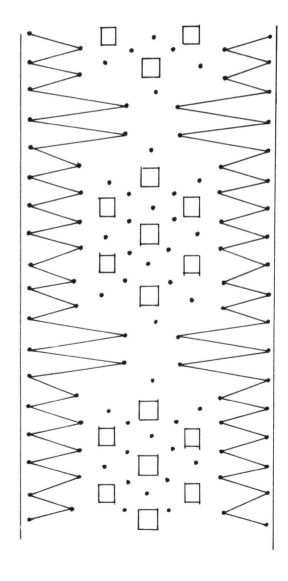

Figure 64. *(Above) The sequence of the pairs in this sample is, from left to right: two natural, two orange, three natural, a pair consisting of one orange and one red thread, two natural, a pair consisting of one orange and one green thread, three natural, two orange, and two natural.*

Figure 65. *(Right) Although the sample seems complex at first glance, the basic pattern is quite simple.*

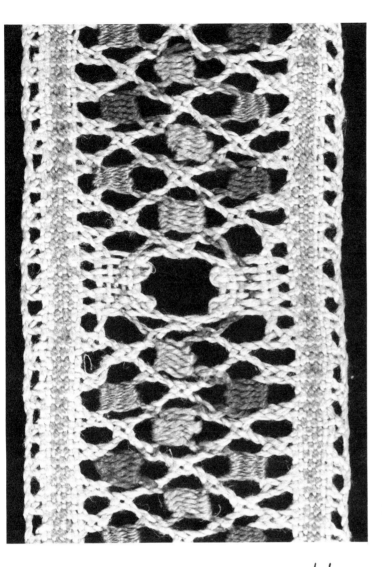

Figure 66. *This sample shows very well how rich lace can be with the tasteful use of colored threads.*

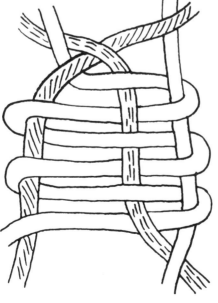

Figure 67. *In order to be able to make alternately colored leadwork squares, the colored threads must cross over each other in the previous leadwork like this.*

METALLIC THREAD

The stiffness of the metallic thread dictates to some degree the stitches used and the design made with them. Metallic threads can be bent in very sharp angles, almost folded and tightly packed together, which suggests that they are particularly suitable for leadwork. The threads can also be bent in very mild curves and used more for long wavy lines than for intricate, closely worked grounds. So, for example, the maiden's net ground is highly unsuitable for the metallic threads, while the loosely worked torchon ground and half stitch ground can be worked successfully.

The sample in Figures 68, 69, and 70 is worked in gold-colored, metallic threads of two different thicknesses—three thick gimp threads and seven pairs of thin metallic thread. The dense, central curved strip is worked as a leadwork using three pairs of bobbins instead of the usual two pairs (see Figure 71). Periodically, the weaving thread of the leadwork twists together with the thread on either edge of the leadwork to work as a pair around the gimp. The pair twists twice, loops around a pin, and twists again after enclosing the gimp.

Then, one of the threads weaves through the rest of the passive threads, while the other thread of the pair becomes one of the passives. As the working drawing shows, some of the pairs are worked in the leadwork strip while others are woven out and used in other parts of the piece. This is done in such a way that every time a new pair enters the leadwork, a pair at the opposite side leaves; thus the leadwork never uses more or less than three pairs at one time.

Working with wire is very similar to working with metallic threads, except that very fine wires are fragile and thick ones are hard to bend. Therefore, the design should be simpler and looser than the designs for the metallic threads.

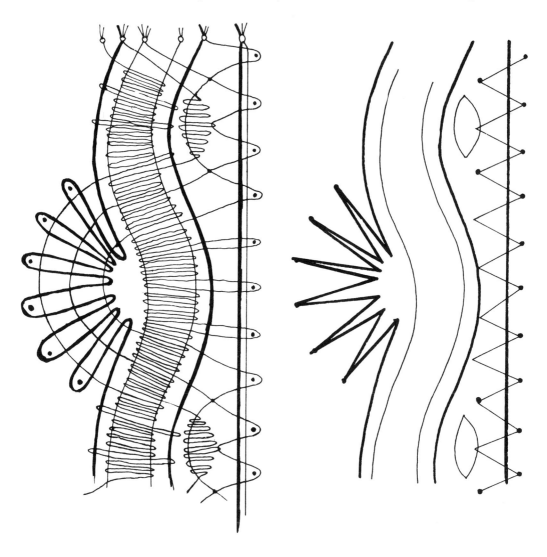

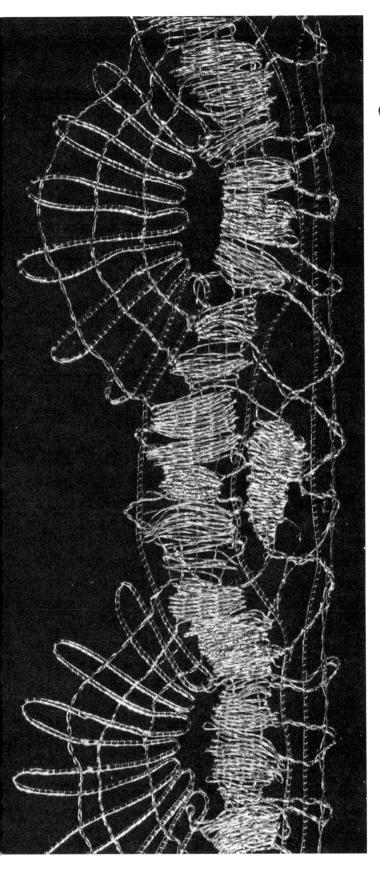

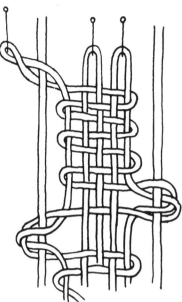

Figure 68. *(Opposite page left) Draft for a sample worked with two different thicknesses of gold-colored metallic threads.*

Figure 69. *(Opposite page right) The pattern for this sample shows that only two stitches—whole stitch and leadwork—are used; yet, in combination with gimps, these two stitches produce a lace with great variety.*

Figure 70. *(Left) The metallic threads, whether they are made with pure metal or plastic, are very bright and shiny and add delicacy to the finished lace.*

Figure 71. *(Above) Three pairs of bobbins work the central strip of leadwork between the two thick gimp threads. At regular intervals, the weaving thread of the leadwork twists together with the outside thread of the leadwork; these two threads work as a pair around the gimp as illustrated in this drawing.*

DESIGNING STRAIGHT LACE

Now that you have completed the straight lace samples, you have a good working knowledge of how to make a piece of lace. In the course of working, you have probably learned about the properties of the materials used, some technical possibilities and limitations, and the esthetic qualities of lace. Now it is time to make the transition from following a pre-designed pattern to designing your own lace. The first step is to design your own lace edgings or insertions in patterns similar to the ones you just completed. Vary the combinations of stitches and the shapes and develop a motif that you repeat regularly. On the next design, allow yourself more freedom. Do not be concerned about repeating motifs, and make a pattern that includes only very basic information. This way you will be guided by the pattern, but you will also be free to change stitches and details of the composition as you are making the lace. See Figure 73 for an idea of what a beginning

lacemaker made following this method.

After you do this successfully, the next step is to design a complete lace, small and simple, composed of stitches you learned and using whatever subject matter you choose. To see how other beginning lacemakers have approached this phase of designing, see Figure 74.

When you complete these first three steps, you are ready to design a larger, more complex lace composed of several units,

Figure 72. *(Right) Dagmar Pilarova made this lace, which illustrates a folk theme in three sections that were later sewn together. Courtesy Jarmila Sikytova, photo V.S.U.P.*

Figure 73. *(Below) Placement edging made by Ludmila Krecanova. Courtesy Jarmila Sikytova, photo V.S.U.P.*

Figure 74. Prague Motifs *(Below right)—lace made in the lacemaking studio of the College of Applied Arts in Prague, Czechoslovakia. Courtesy Jarmila Sikytova, photo V.S.U.P.*

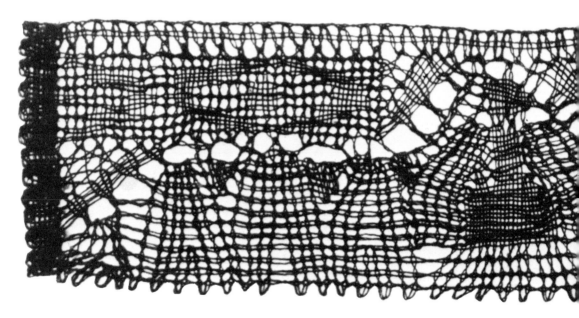

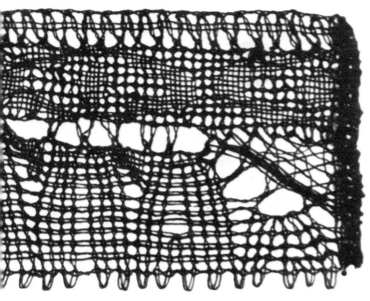

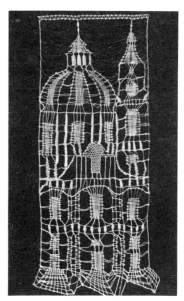

such as the laces shown in Figures 72 and 75. These particular examples were too wide to be worked on an ordinary pillow—they were worked in sections and then sewn together. This does not mean that they could not be worked in any other way—a Spanish cylindrical pillow could have been used if the lace were not so wide, or a very long cylindrical pillow could have been made especially for such a lace. It is also possible to work lace sideways—the only drawback is that you must view your composition from the side. This would probably necessitate turning the pillow quite often to gain a proper perspective of what you are doing. Also, rather than make such a wide lace, you could create a long lace with a vertical composition to eliminate the need for making the lace in sections.

When making these laces, feel free to use various thicknesses and types of thread (see Figure 76). If you want to use color, use it sparingly at first. Actually, the same is true of the use of stitches. Intricate combinations of stitches and/or colors require a great deal of planning, and, although you should not be discouraged by this, you ought to work up to complex designs gradually.

As you make more and more laces, you will get a better idea of how to select the material to

be used. The stiffness of wire, for example, can be used to form the basic structure of a crown or another self-supported three-dimensional form. On the other hand, the sharpness of the ends of the wire may preclude its use as a comfortable garment. Remember, though, that these are only considerations—not obstacles. By becoming aware of them, you will be freer to use lace to its fullest potential.

Figure 75. (Above) This lace, based on a folk dancing theme, was also made in parts that were later sewn together. It was made by a student at the College of Applied Arts in Prague, Czechoslovakia. Courtesy Jarmila Sikytova, photo V.S.U.P.

Figure 76. (Left) Detail of a compositional lace study incorporating varying thicknesses of threads made by Emilie Frydecka. Courtesy Jarmila Sikytova, photo V.S.U.P.

TAPE LACE

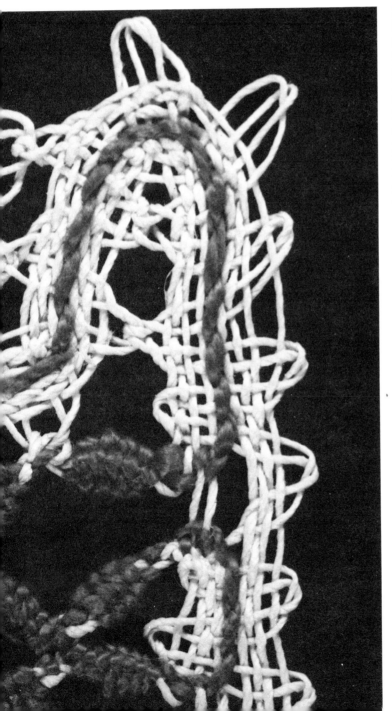

Because only a small number of bobbins and a relatively few basic stitches are used in making tape lace, this type of lace lends itself well to the beginning lacemaker. At the same time, tape lace offers exciting possibilities, some of which are evident in the Russian tape laces pictured in this section and at the beginning of the book. Drafting patterns for tape lace is quite simple—all that is needed on the pattern is the outline of the tape showing its width and direction and the path of the leader pair. You do not need a pricking, since pins are only used at the edges of the lace.

The difference between a lace fabric of the same size made by straight lace and tape lace is the number of bobbins used. A large piece of straight lace may use a few hundred bobbins, whereas the same-sized piece of tape lace can be made from one, two, or perhaps three tapes, each with a maximum of twelve pairs of bobbins.

The most sophisticated use of tapes is in Russian laces. In these laces, not only do the tapes wind in all directions—and connect with each other where they meet—but the same threads used to make the tapes leave the tapes long enough to form the filling ground before returning to the tapes.

TYPES OF TAPES

There are many kinds of tape lace—I will describe the simplest types first and then go on to the more complex ones.

Sample One. The most basic tape used in tape laces is nothing more than the linen stitch sample described on page 56. This sample (see Figures 1 and 4) is made with four passive pairs and one leader pair. The edges on this tape—as well as on many other tapes—are looped, which facilitates the process of connecting tapes together.

Sample Two. Although this tape is only slightly different than the first sample in its construction, it has a more open, airy feeling (see Figures 2 and 4). The difference is that in addition to the core of linen stitches, this sample has a pair of bobbins on each side done in the whole stitch.

To make the sample, use pair 1 as a leader and make a whole stitch with pair 2. Continuing with the leader, make a linen stitch with pair 3 and then pair 4. Before making the whole stitch with pair 5, twist the leader. After completing the whole stitch with pair 5, turn the leader around a pin, make an additional twist, and work back to the left edge in the same way. By repeating this cycle, you can produce the desired length of tape.

Sample Three. To make the tape just completed in the sec-ond sample wider, just add more passive pairs. You may use as many bobbins as you wish in a tape, but ten or twelve pairs is usually as many as can be comfortably handled. When you use more than ten or twelve pairs, the leader begins to sag, since no pins are used in the interior portion of the tape. Also, the tape becomes too wide to curve easily. In this sample (see Figures 3 and 4), seven pairs of bobbins are worked in the same way as in Sample Two. Pair 1 is the leader again, and, after making a whole stitch with pair 2 and linen stitches with pairs 3 and 4, it twists. Then the leader makes linen stitches with pairs 5 and 6, twists, and works a whole stitch with pair 7.

Figure 1. *Pattern for Sample One. This tape, made with the linen stitch, is the most basic of all the lace tapes.*

Figure 2. *The pattern for the second sample indicates the direction of the tape, the leader, and the position of the pins.*

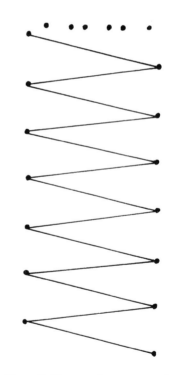

Figure 3. *The use of seven pairs of bobbins makes this third sample wider than the previous two. Ten or twelve pairs are usually the maximum number for a tape—the leader would tend to sag if there were more, since it is held only by pins at the edges of the tape.*

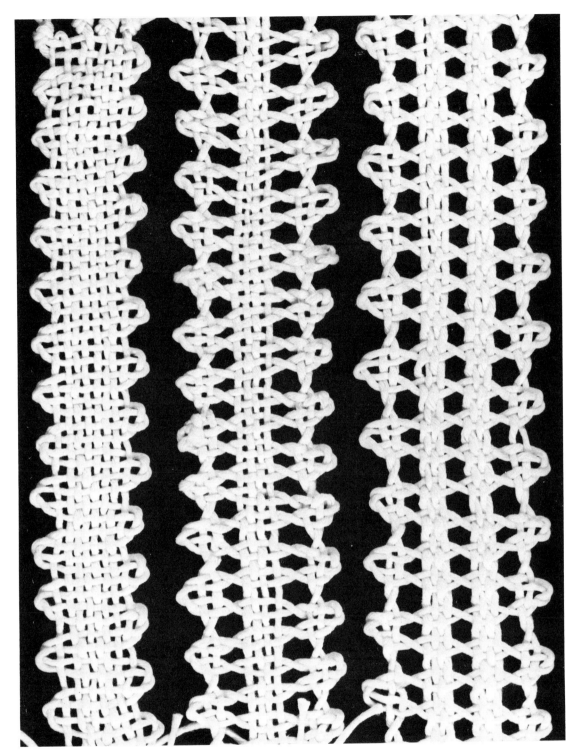

Figure 4. *From left to right: completed Samples One, Two, and Three. Note the progression from a dense tape (Sample One) to a tape with a much more open feeling (Sample Three).*

Sample Four. The tape laces in this sample and in Samples 5 and 6 are more decorative than those in the first three samples. In fact, they are as complex as tapes can be without having to use pins in the interior of the tape while it is being made.

This sample uses seven passive pairs—three central pairs and two pairs at each edge—plus one leader pair. By twisting the leader pair between the edge pairs and the central pairs, the space between them is accentuated (see Figures 5 and 8). The leader begins at the left-hand side. After working to the right edge and turning around the pin, it works back toward the left—but only through pairs 7 through 3 (omitting pairs 1 and 2). Then the leader twists twice and works back to the right edge through pairs 3 through 7. By not placing a pin at this turn, the central pairs 3, 4, and 5 are all pulled over to the right edge, leaving an open space on the left.

Insert a pin at the right edge, work the leader all the way to the left edge, and insert another pin. Now the leader moves in the same sequence as it did before in reverse—working through pairs 2 through 6 and back to the left edge to create the opening on the right side of the lace. Thus the openings alternate, and the middle part of the tape curves from side to side.

When the central three pairs are pulled to one side just once by the leader pair, the result is a rather tight curve. More gradual curves are possible by making the leader pull the central three pairs to one side more than once in succession.

Sample Five. This tape has small, regularly spaced openings created by exchanging a leader with one of the passive pairs (see Figures 6 and 8). There are five passive pairs and one leader pair. The three central passive pairs are worked in linen stitch, while each of the passive pairs at the edge are worked in a whole stitch. When you make this sample, always twist the leader after it works the three central pairs.

Begin the sample by working the leader to the right edge. Turn it around a pin in a looped edge, and work back to the left edge. Again turn the leader around a pin in a loop edge, and work it toward the right—but only through pairs 2 and 3. At this point, drop the leader pair, which becomes a passive pair, and pick up pair 4. Pair 4 becomes the leader and works all the way to the right edge, then all the way to the left, and back again to the right edge. After turning around the pin, it works toward the left through pairs 6 and 5. Now you should drop the leader and pick up pair 4 (which was the original leader pair). It becomes the leader again, working all the way to the left edge. Continue to work the sample this way until it is completed.

Sample Six. This sample is as complex a tape as can be made easily without running into technical difficulties. This particular pattern lends itself very well for use as an edging or insertion. It is made with six pairs, four of which alternate in assuming the role of leader. Out of the original six pairs only pairs 2 and 5 remain passive throughout the entire tape. All stitches made in the sample are whole stitches, and every pair makes a double twist as it travels across the center of the lace, separating the two sides of the tape (see Figures 7 and 8). Please note that more than two or three twists by pairs in the center of the lace will weaken the structure of the lace.

To begin the sample, use pair 1 as the leader and work through pairs 2, 3, and 4 with the whole stitch. Next, work pair 6 through pair 5 and then pair 4. Work pair 2 through pairs 3, 4, 5, and 6, turn around a pin, and work back with pair 2 through pairs 6, 5, and 4. Next, work pair 2 to the left through pair 1, around a pin, and back through pairs 1 and 3. Pick up pair 5, and work toward the left through pairs 4, 3, 2, and 1. After you turn around the pin, you are ready to repeat the whole sequence again in the second unit. This may sound confusing to you, but if you read these instructions carefully before you begin, and try to follow the action through the drawings, you will gain an understanding of the procedure. When you actually start the lace, you will see that the sequence is quite simple.

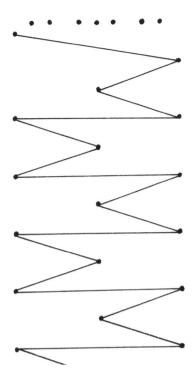

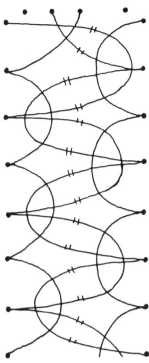

Figure 5. *Pattern for Sample Four. By twisting the leader pair between the edge pairs and the central pairs, subtle changes in the tape begin to take place—such as the curving of the central strip.*

Figure 6. *The small, regularly spaced openings in this sample are created by exchanging the leader with one of the passive pairs, as the pattern indicates.*

Figure 7. *This rather complex sample is made entirely by whole stitches with six pairs, four of which alternate as leaders. The series of small lines down the center of the pattern represents a double twist.*

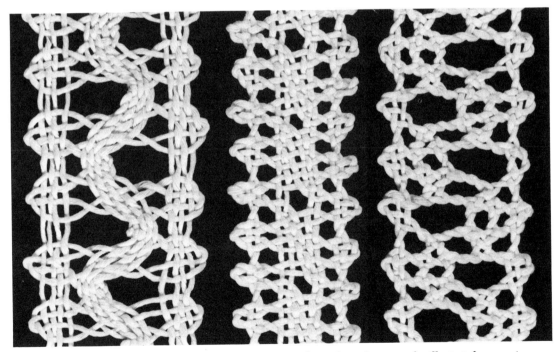

Figure 8. *From left to right: completed Samples Four, Five, and Six. These three samples illustrate how maximum variety can be achieved by the use of simple techniques. More complex tapes are possible, but they present numerous technical problems.*

There are times when a tape is intended for the edge of a work, and you may want a fancy scallop for that edge. The following two samples are common ways to make these scalloped edges.

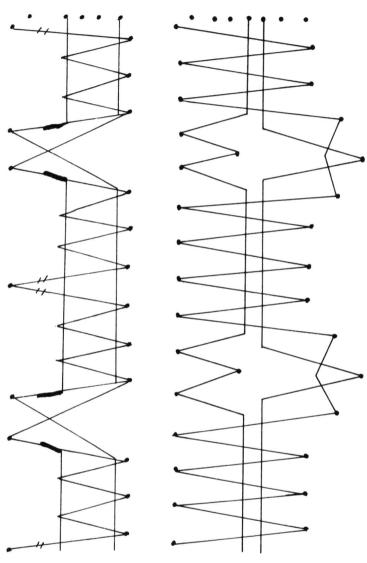

Figure 9. *As this pattern indicates, this sample is very open. When it is worked on a curve, however, the spaces along the foot at the left diminish in size, causing the foot to become more substantial than it appears here.*

Figure 10. *Pattern for a fancy scallop along the head of lace to be used as an edging. Note that the process creates large openings.*

Sample One. This sample tape (see Figures 9 and 11) may seem rather sparse at its foot edge, but since it is usually made on a curve with the foot edge as the smaller radius of the curve, the stitches and twists there become quite a bit denser. The sample is worked straight here, with six passive pairs and the leader always forming looped edges on both sides of the tape. Begin by working leader pair 1 through pair 2 in a whole stitch. Add an extra twist to the leader pair before going on to make linen stitches with pairs 3, 4, and 5. Then, the leader and pair 6 form a whole stitch. Work the leader toward the left through pairs 5, 4, 3, and 2, turn without inserting a pin, and work the leader back through these pairs to the right edge. Repeat this sequence.

Work the leader pair back toward the left through pairs 5, 4, and 3. Then make a braid about half the distance to pair 1 with the leader and pair 2. Twist the leader, weave through pair 1, and turn and work pair 1 all the way to the right until it works through pair 5. The leader pair and pair 5 exchange roles, and pair 5 works all the way to the left edge. After turning around the pin, work the new leader through pair 2, and make a braid—the same length as the previous braid—with pair 3.

When you finish the braid, whichever pair is on the right assumes the role of leader. The pair on the left becomes passive pair 2. Work the leader all the way to the right and then back through pair 2. Repeat this right-left sequence once more, and work again to the right edge. This time, when you work the leader to the left, take it all the way through pair 1. Turn around the pin, and you are ready to construct the second unit the same way.

Sample Two. This sample requires eight pairs of bobbins and is also worked with the head of the lace on the right side and the foot on the left side (see Figures 10 and 11). Begin with the leader (pair 1), make a whole stitch with pair 2, linen stitches with pairs 3 through 7, and another whole stitch with pair 8. Make a loop edge around a pin (as you will do throughout the sample), and work in this way back to the left edge, then to the right, left, and right again. Now you are ready to construct the small scallop.

Turn the leader to the left, and work through pairs 7, 6, and 5. Now pair 6 becomes the leader and works to the right through pairs 7 and 8. Turn the leader back toward the left and work through pairs 7, 6, and 5. Pick up the original leader, and form the third loop of the scallop. While all of this is happening, pair 4 becomes a leader itself and works through pairs 1, 2, and 3 to the left, right, left, and right again. Then it again assumes its original role as passive pair 4.

Return to the right side of the tape, and pick up pair 8 (which has just formed the third loop of the scallop). Turn it around the pin, and work it through all pairs to the left edge. Work that pair back and forth through all pairs five more times, until it works to the first loop of the second scallop. The number of times this pair works back and forth is a personal choice—in this sample, it works back and forth six times. Remember that the leader pair always makes whole stitches with the edge pairs and linen stitches with the five central pairs as it works from edge to edge.

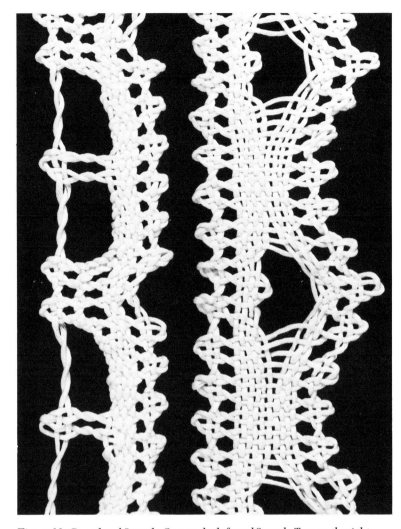

Figure 11. *Completed Sample One on the left and Sample Two on the right. These are only two examples of how to construct tapes intended for use as edgings. Many more could be designed that would be equally effective in creating openings to make the tape more decorative.*

Figure 12. *Five pairs of bobbins worked in linen stitch plus one gimp pair in color make up this sample. The twined gimp—the thick line down the center of the pattern—twists consistently from right to left (see Figure 18 left).*

Figure 13. *At first glance, this pattern looks the same as the pattern in Figure 12, but, if you look closely, you will see that the four dots at the top of the pattern are farther apart. This allows for openings to appear in the tape along the sides of the central strip (see Figure 18 center).*

Figure 14. *This pattern shows seven pairs of bobbins combined with two pairs of twined gimp. The gimp threads twist in opposite directions in the tape (see Figure 18 right).*

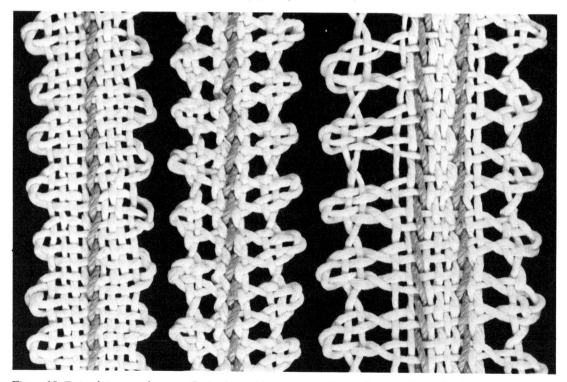

Figure 18. *Twined gimp can be very effectively used in tapes, sometimes relying on their color for contrast, at other times on their thicker diameter, and sometimes both. See Figures 12–14 for the patterns of these tapes.*

 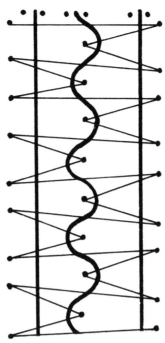 

Figure 15. *A third gimp pair is added in this pattern. The tape is worked in linen stitch, and the gimps can be twisted in either direction—but once the direction is chosen, you cannot change it (see Figure 19 left).*

Figure 16. *This sample used three gimp pairs, one of which curves (see Figure 19 center).*

Figure 17. *By pinning the gimp pairs in a color sequence of yellow, red, red, yellow, and by twisting the gimp pairs toward each other, a chain of links is formed which are alternately red and yellow (see Figure 19 right).*

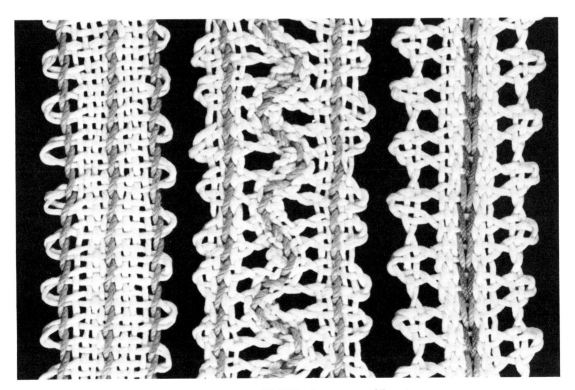

Figure 19. *More uses of gimps in tapes. See Figures 15–17 for the patterns of these tapes.*

GIMP IN TAPES

Twined gimps are the only type of gimp used in tape lace. Since I described them on pages 90–91, I will not repeat their technical construction.

The twined gimp in straight lace is used to accentuate a shape by outlining it or to create a particular shape by its own movement. In tape lace, the gimp runs along the center or edges of the tape with the other threads to stress the directional movement of the threads themselves (see Figures 12–19). The gimp in tape lace stands out because it is raised above the surface.

There can be one, two, or even three gimps in one tape. If they are the same color as the rest of the tape, they rely on their three-dimensionality for effect; if they are colored, that in itself adds a more obvious effect. The laces of Eastern Europe combine bright colors with natural or white. Because linen does not dye well, cotton is used in combination with natural or white linen. The fact that cotton is not as strong or as stiff as linen does not affect the structural soundness of the finished lace when it is used for the gimp. Traditionally, the primary colors were most commonly used, but you are by no means restricted to those colors. Usually, the threads of a gimp pair are of the same color, but in some cases each thread of a pair is a different color.

CURVING TAPES

Curving tapes present no particular problems, but there are various ways to work curves, some of which will be described now. The most important fact to keep in mind about curved tapes is that the circumferences of the inner and outer edges of the curve differ a lot. Thus the threads are more compressed at the inner portion of the curve than they are at the outer edges. When working these tapes, you should try to rotate your pillow to keep the leader horizontal and the passive pairs basically vertical. This way the lace will always be in its normal working position.

Sample One. This is the simplest way to handle a curved tape (see Figures 20 and 21). The sample is made in linen stitch with looped edges with six pairs of bobbins, pair 1 being the leader. As you work the sample, you will see that the loops along the inner curve of the tape are much closer together than the loops along the outer edge.

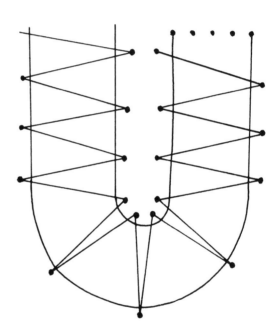

Figure 20. *The sample done entirely in linen stitch with six pairs of bobbins is worked over a pattern such as this.*

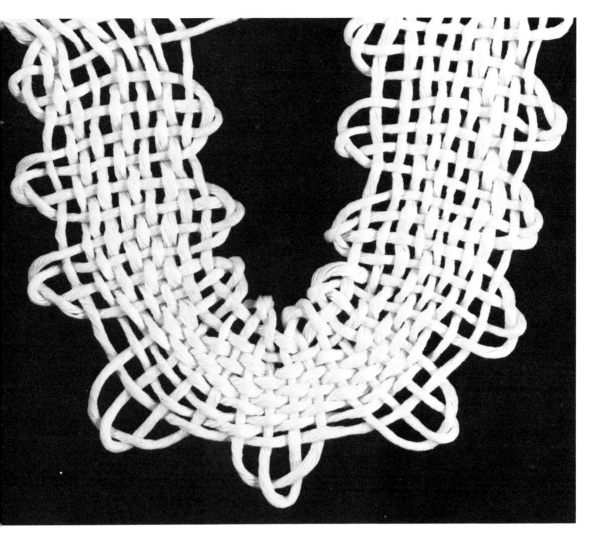

Figure 21. *Sample One—the way the curve is handled here is one of the simplest and most basic methods. You just make the lace denser on the inner part of the curve than on the outside edge.*

Sample Two. This sample (see Figures 22 and 23) is also worked with six pairs of bobbins in linen stitch with looped edges, except here pairs 1 and 2 alternate as leaders in the curve. This results in a tape that is less crowded along its inside edge. Proceed in the same way as you did in the first sample, working the leader to the right, left, right, and left again. At this point pair 2 takes over as the leader, and you work it first to the right and then back to the left, where pair 1 again assumes the leader role. Work pair 1 to the right and back to the left. Then exchange pairs, and work pair 2 to the right and back to the left. Pick up pair 1, and continue working back and forth from left to right edge with this pair until you complete the sample.

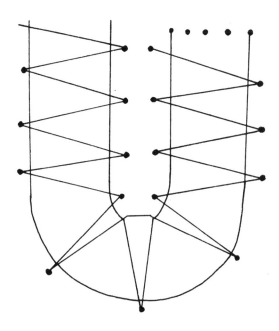

Figure 22. *(Above) Pattern for Sample Two—pairs 1 and 2 exchange roles as leaders in the curve.*

Figure 23. *(Below) Sample Two—the inner edge of the curve is less crowded.*

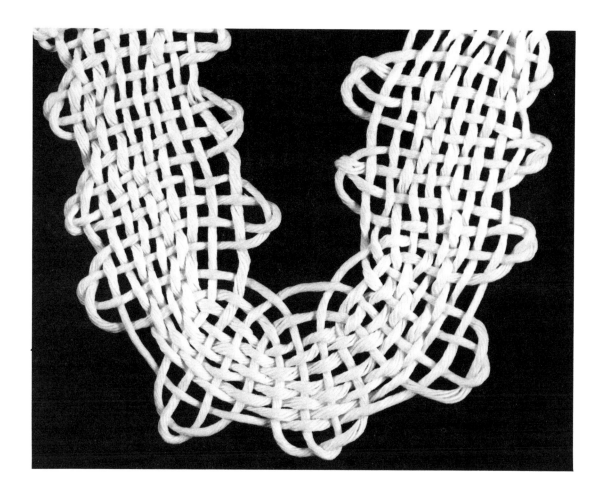

Sample Three. Again six pairs of bobbins form this sample (see Figures 24 and 25), but only the central three pairs are worked in linen stitch—pairs 2 and 6 are worked in the whole stitch, and pairs 1 and 3 alternate as leaders. Begin the same way you began the first two samples, working the leader pair to the right and left, twice. Then go to the right and back toward the left through pair 3, omitting pair 1. Pick up pair 3, and, using it as a leader, work to the right edge and back to the left, again omitting pair 1. With the original leader, work to the right edge and back to the left through pair 2. Next, work pair 3 to the right and then to the left through pair 2. Using the original leader, work to the outside edge and then to the left edge through pair 1. Continue with this leader until the sample is complete.

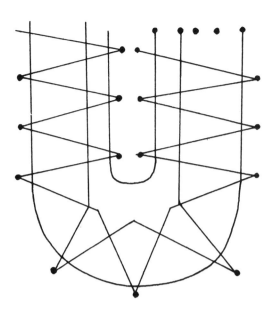

Figure 24. *(Above) This pattern shows six pairs of bobbins again. Only the central three pairs are worked in the linen stitch, while pairs 2 and 6 are worked in the whole stitch.*

Figure 25. *(Below) Sample Three—by working the tape this way, you produce a curve that is uncluttered and handsome.*

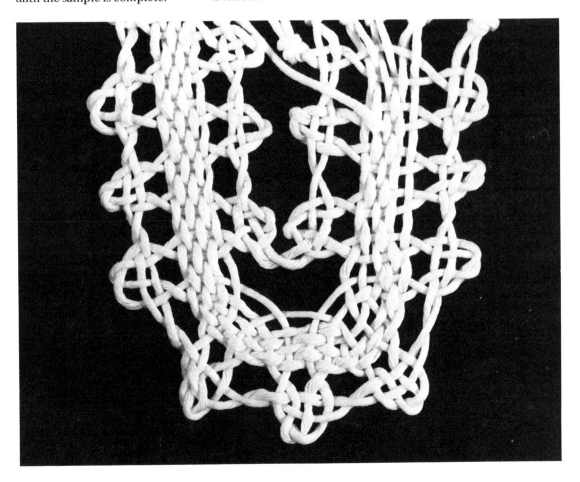

Sample Four. This curve, not as sharp as the ones in the previous samples, creates an opening in the center which alleviates the problem of overcrowding and makes it possible to work the tape the same way that you did in Sample One. This sample (see Figures 26 and 27) uses six pairs of bobbins and is worked entirely in linen stitch with loops at the edges. Pair 1 is the only leader throughout.

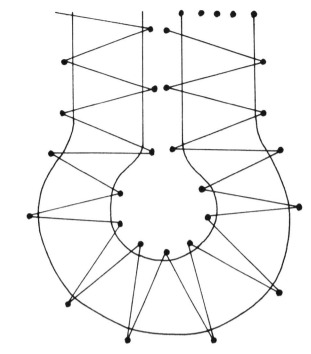

Figure 26. *(Top right) Six pairs are used in this sample, which is worked entirely in linen stitch with looped edges.*

Figure 27. *Sample Four—a more uniform spacing of the stitches results from widening the swing of the tape in the curve.*

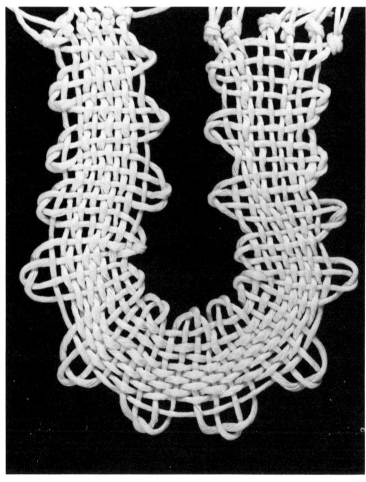

Sample Five. This is one of the most common ways to work a right-angle curve in a tape (see Figures 28 and 29). Use six pairs of bobbins again and work the sample in the linen stitch with loop edges. Begin the sample by working the leader pair 1 back and forth twice, ending up at the left edge of the tape. Then work pair 2 to the right edge and back to the left, but not through pair 1. Pick up pair 3 and do the same, but when working to the left omit pairs 1 and 2. Work pairs 4 and 5 in the same manner. To work the second half of the curve, repeat the same procedure in reverse, working pairs 4, 3, 2, and at last the original leader pair through the passive pairs.

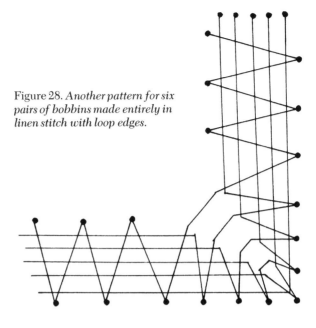

Figure 28. *Another pattern for six pairs of bobbins made entirely in linen stitch with loop edges.*

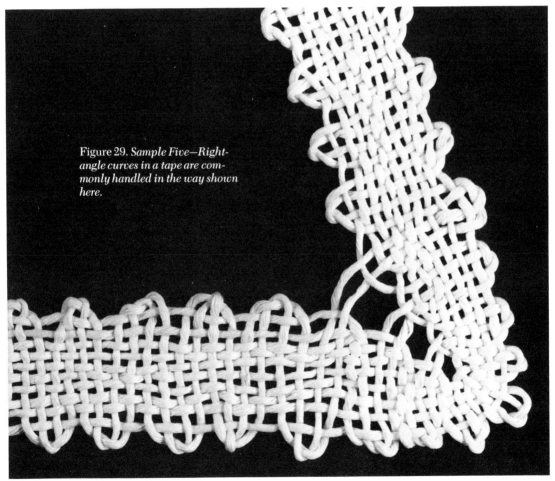

Figure 29. *Sample Five—Right-angle curves in a tape are commonly handled in the way shown here.*

CROCEHTAGE, OR SEWING TAPES

When you use tapes to form a fabric, they wind and curve all about. In order to give this fabric structural soundness, these tapes must be connected where they meet. The method used to connect these tapes is called crochetage, or sewing. To do this you can use a pin—there is always one close by—but a crochet hook is better. You need different size hooks for the various thicknesses of threads, but if you buy three sizes of hooks, you will probably satisfy any need. If the hook is too large, it will not go through the loop at the edge of the tape; if it is too small, it will not be able to hold the entire thread, and the hook will thus tend to split the thread. As metal hooks hold up better than plastic hooks, I suggest you use only metal ones.

Sample One. The process of sewing tapes is very simple and should present no problems for you. One way to do it is as follows (see Figure 30). As the leader pair approaches an edge loop of the tape you are making, insert your crochet hook from the top side of the tape through an edge loop of the tape already made and catch one of the threads of the leader pair. Pull the thread through the edge loop, forming a large loop that is big enough to allow the bobbin carrying the remaining thread of the leader pair to be pushed through handle first. Then, pull both bobbins gently, so the loop on one of the leaders closes. Twist the leader pair, and proceed weaving back into the tape. The length of the edge loops and of the leaders sewing into them is equal—thus the sewing ends up in the center of the two tapes (see Figures 31 and 32).

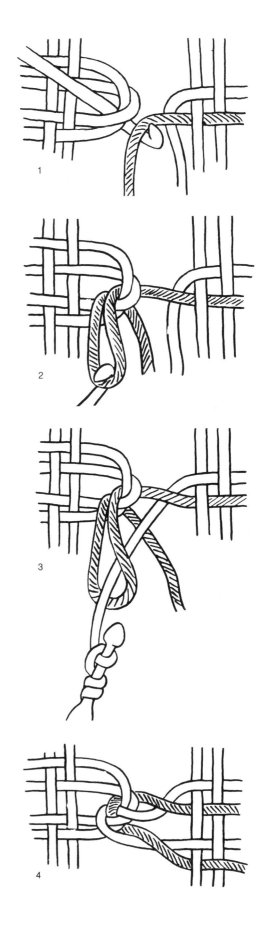

Figure 30. *(Left) Sewing one tape to another: (1) Insert your crochet hook through the edge loop of the existing tape and hook one of the threads of the leader pair of the tape you are making. (2) Pull the thread through the edge loop, making a loop large enough for a bobbin to pass through. (3) Pass the other bobbin of the leader pair through the loop. (4) Pull the bobbins gently to close the loop and firm the stitch; then twist this leader pair and continue working on the tape.*

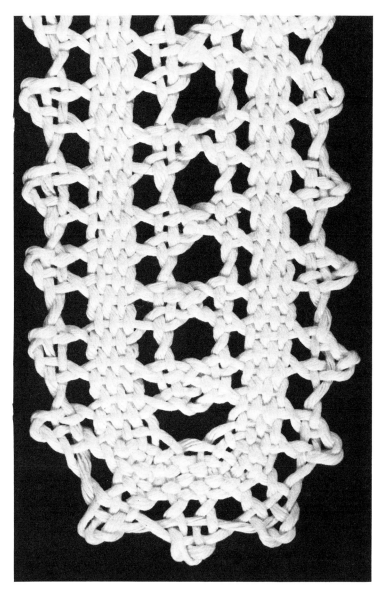

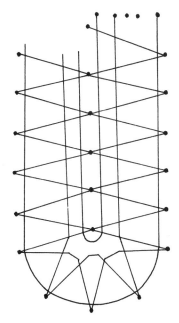

Figure 31. *Pattern for sewing tapes together.*

Figure 32. *Sample One—one method of sewing tapes together— since the lengths of the edge loops and of the leaders sewing into them are equal, the sewing is centered between the two tapes.*

Sample Two. If you want more space between the two tapes, you can keep the edge loop small and twist the leader pair several times before sewing it through this edge loop (see Figures 33 and 34). The actual sewing, then, lies off center, and the space between the tapes is wider.

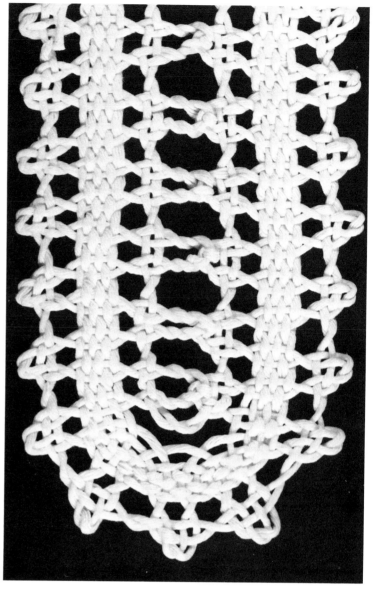

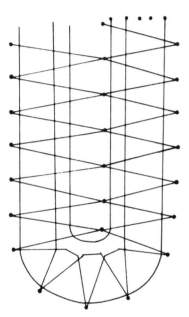

Figure 33. *Pattern for tape to be sewn together—the center strip of this sample is worked in linen stitch, while pairs 2 and 6 are worked in whole stitch.*

Figure 34. *Sample Two—by twisting the leader pair several times before actually sewing, open spaces are created in the center of the lace, and the sewing is off center.*

Sample Three. There are times when more than one loop has to be sewn at one time (see Figures 35 and 36). In this sample, two tapes expand to form a circle, the center of which is divided into four segments. Every fifth loop extends to the center to form these segments. The procedure for sewing all of these loops together is to place a pin in the center of the circle and loop the first three extended loops around it. As you make the fourth and final loop, remove the pin, insert the crochet hook in its place through the three loops, and sew all the loops together.

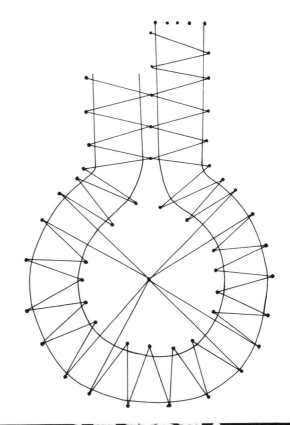

Figure 35. *(Top right) Pattern for tape expanded to form a circle. The central portion is divided into four segments by extending every fifth loop to the center. The first three loops are all sewn together by the fourth loop.*

Figure 36. *Sample Three—this tape permits large negative spaces while retaining its structural integrity.*

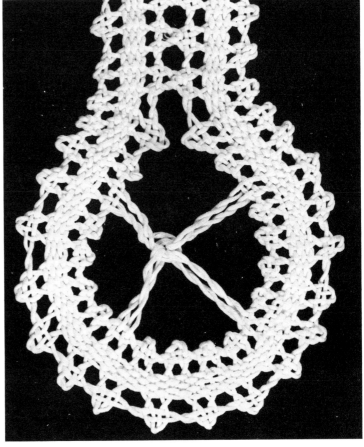

Sample Four. Another place to use the same technique as in Sample Three is in a single tape that makes a wide radius at the curve (see Figures 37 and 38). Both the extended loops and the sewing add structural strength to the curved tape. There is no set rule dictating how many loops you should bring into the center, but you must bring enough to make the unit structurally sound.

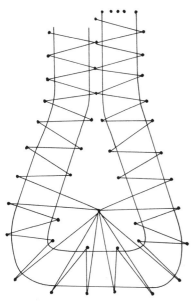

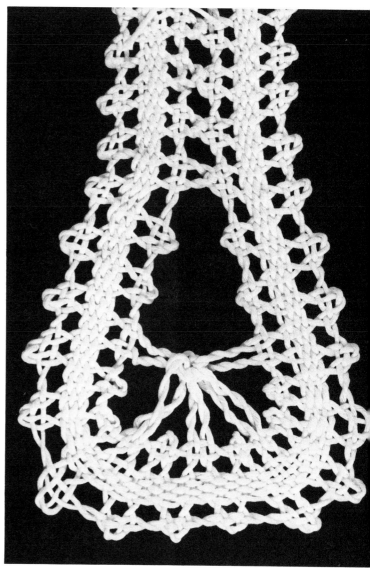

Figure 37. *When the lace makes a wide radius at the curve, loops are brought into the center and sewn together as indicated in this pattern.*

Figure 38. *Sample Four—any number of loops can be extended to the center and sewn so long as there are enough to retain a sound structure.*

Sample Five. Some circular forms made by a tape are so large in diameter and have so many loops coming to the center that sewing them together in one place would produce a very bulky knot. Such is the case in this sample, where six loops are brought into the central portion of the circle formed by the tape (see Figures 39 and 40). To avoid the bulky knot, these loops go only part way into the center, and each one turns around a separate pin.

When you reach point F in Figure 39 with the leader pair, twist the pair once and loop the threads around a pin. Remove the pin from the loop at point A and insert the crochet hook through this loop. Hook one thread of the leader pair, pull it through the loop, and allow it to hang loose. Remove the hook from the loop at point A and put it through the loop at point B, after removing the pin there. Hook the same loop you pulled through loop A, and pull it through the loop at point B. Allow it to hang loose and go on to the loop at points C, D, and E. To keep the lace even, replace the pins after completing the sewing at each point.

After pulling the leader thread through the loop at point E, hook the threads of the leader pair one at a time and pull the bobbins through this loop. Tighten the threads, twist them, and go back to the tape.

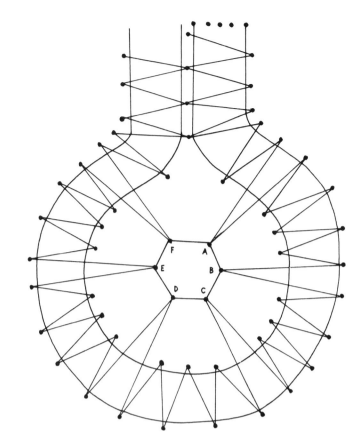

Figure 39. *(Top right) The loops here extend only part way into the center of the opening. When the last loop is formed at point F, it is drawn through all the other loops until it comes back to point F— where it is sewn to itself.*

Figure 40. *Sample Five—the substructure created within the opening takes the place of the knot in Sample Four.*

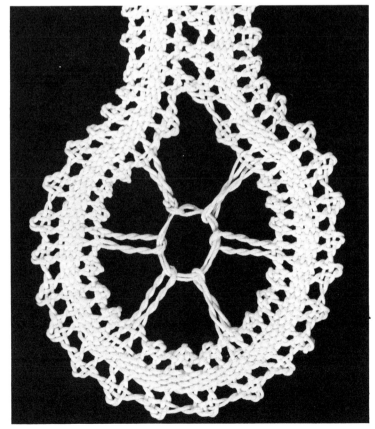

Sample Six. This sample and the one following should give you a better idea of how to combine the tapes by sewing. One of the most basic curving patterns in tape lace, it is a beautiful edging composed of identical repeating curves (see Figures 41 and 42). You can make it as long as you like, and you can use it in many ways.

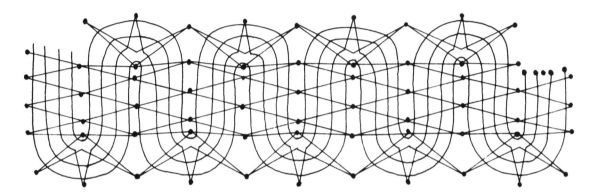

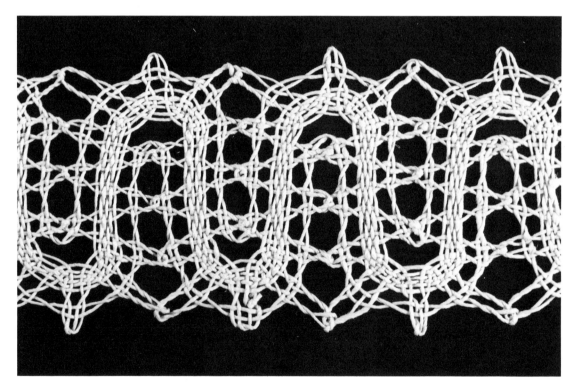

Figure 41. *(Top) This is a pattern for one of the most basic curving tape motifs. As you work it, you should rotate the pillow so the leader is always worked horizontally.*

Figure 42. *(Above) Sample Six— these repeating motifs could be continued indefinitely to form any length of edging desired.*

Sample Seven. This flower motif combines all the sewing techniques you just learned (see Figures 43 and 44).

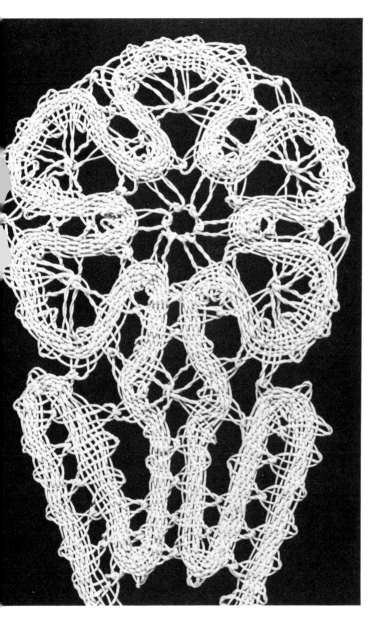

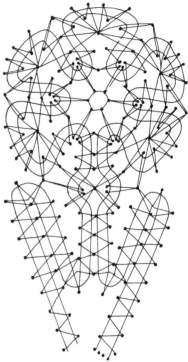

Figure 43. *The pattern for this project looks quite complex, but it actually contains simple units, all of which are presented in this section on tape lace.*

Figure 44. *Sample Seven—the finished flower motif shows how effectively you can combine different sewing techniques in a single lace.*

CROSSING TAPES

There are times when tapes cross each other in a pattern. In fact, some tape laces are composed entirely of curling tapes that cross each other constantly. In order to create a structural solidity in these laces, the place where the two tapes cross must be sewn using the technique described above.

In the sample (see Figures 45 and 46), the two overlapping tapes are sewn together at points, A, B, C, and D. As you can see, the pattern has been drafted so that the turns of the leader pair meet at these four corners. You must do this if you are going to sew the tape together. Begin working the tape from the top, and go around the curve to the right until you reach point A with the leader pair. Remove the pin from the loop at the edge of the tape at point A, and sew the leader pair into this loop as described on pages 122–123. Continue with the leader pair to point B and do the same thing. Work the leader back and forth to point C and again sew the leader to the loop there. Proceed to point D and repeat the process. Continue to work the tape in the usual manner after the crossing is completed.

The project in Figures 47 and 48 contains crossing tapes and is an edging using a common motif found in tape laces. You can make it as long as you like.

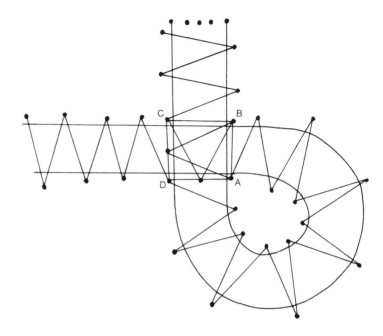

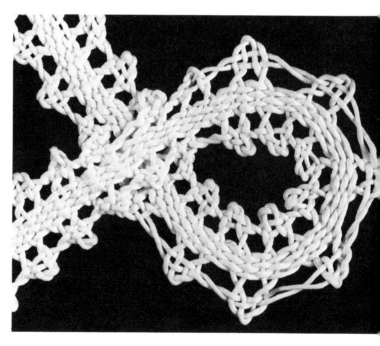

Figure 45. *(Top) In this sample, the two tapes are sewn where they cross at points A, B, C, and D in the pattern in that sequence.*

Figure 46. *(Above) Structural soundness dictates that crossing tapes be sewn together like this.*

Figure 47. *(Top right) This pattern contains two repeating motifs, but you can make any number of them.*

Figure 48. *(Right) This typical edging motif illustrates how effective crossing tapes can be.*

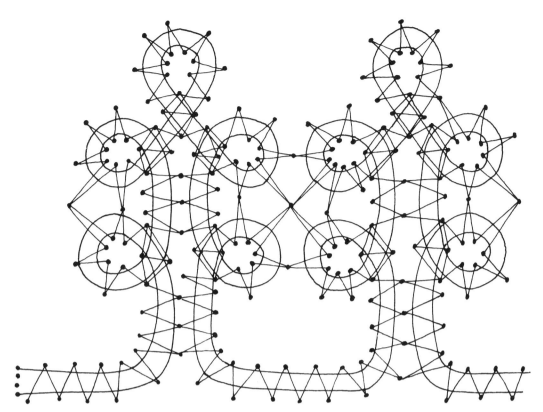

TAPE GROUNDS

There are a number of ways to create a ground or ground effect using tapes, and I describe one of these ways here in two samples. A tape that is worked in a dense stitch (in these cases the linen stitch), changes to a much more open stitch (the Brussels ground or half stitch here), makes a section of tape that appears to be a ground, and goes back to the dense stitch.

Sample One. As you can see, a very beautiful and effective lace of this type can be produced from a simple zigzag pattern (see Figures 49 and 50). The rows of semicircles along the edges are formed by the linen stitch, while the central portion of the lace formed by the straight tapes sewn together gives the impression of a solid mesh worked in one piece.

Begin at the upper left-hand corner with six pairs of bobbins, and work the tape toward the bottom in the same way as you did in Sample Six on page 111. After completing the straight part of the tape, work the leader through all pairs in linen stitch—forming a foot edge on the inner side and a looped edge on the outer side of the curve. When you complete the curve, work the straight portion again. As you go along, sew it to the other straight part of the tape you just made. Repeat the process of changing from one stitch to the other until the sample is complete.

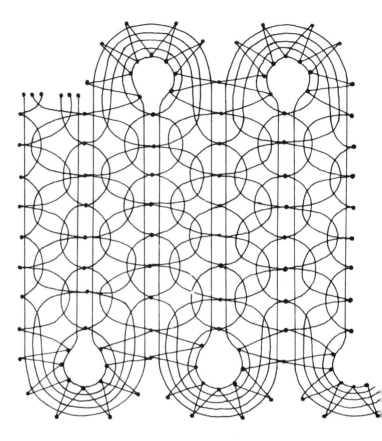

Figure 49. *(Above) This simple zig-zag pattern results in an effective tape ground.*

Figure 50. *(Right) Sample One—the lace is very strong and durable, though wide and open.*

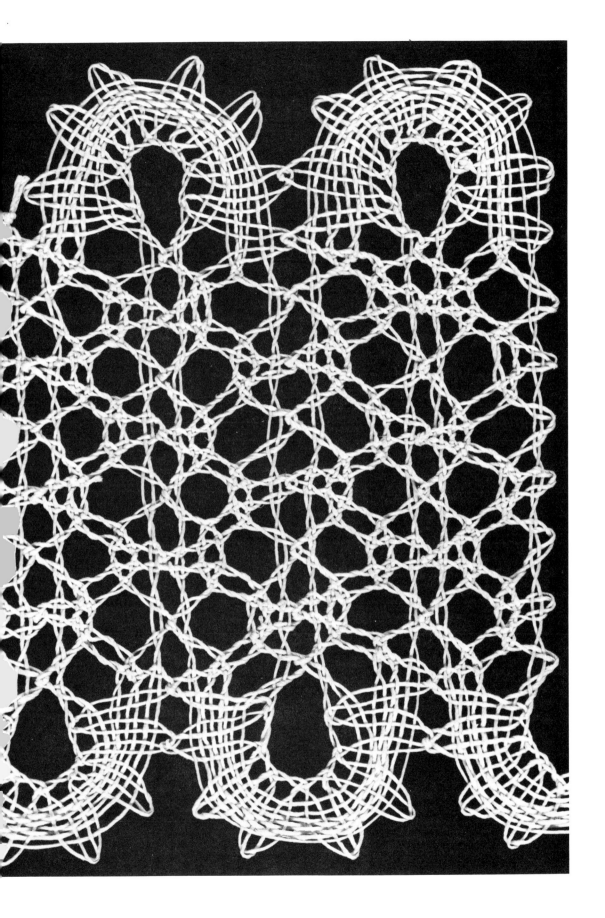

Sample Two. This sample of a section of edging is made with a tape worked alternately in linen stitch and half stitch (see Figures 51 and 52). If you were working a long strip of this edging, you would work the thin tape along the top of the lace at the same time you worked the body of the tape. You would use one set of bobbins for the narrow tape along the top edge,

and another set for the remainder of the lace.

However, since you are only working a small section of lace, you can work it in one piece—make the top, straight strip of tape first, from right to left. Then form a curve and work the tape (still in linen stitch) through the central part of the motif, making sure to sew the tapes together along their inside

edges. Next, expand the tape into a rather loosely worked half stitch. Work it around the linen stitch tape you just completed, again sewing the two tapes together as you go. Change back to linen stitch when the pattern indicates that you should. To create an interesting edge, work the edge in the way described in Sample Two on page 112.

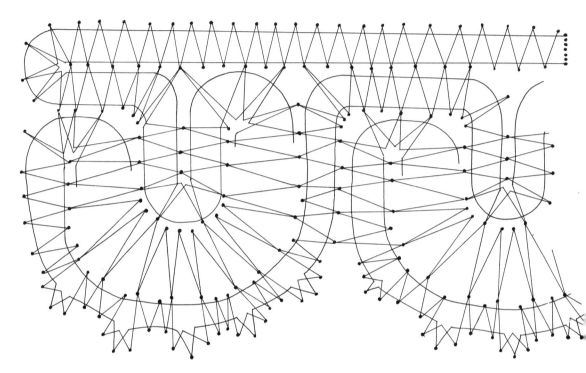

Figure 51. *(Above) This pattern shows that eight pairs of bobbins make this sample. The bobbins combine linen stitch and half stitch to form a wide edging.*

Figure 52. *(Above right) Sample Two—the same bobbins used to make the main, lower portion of the lace are also used to make the thin strip of lace along the top edge of the sample. If several repeats were going to be made, this thin strip would be worked with another set of bobbins.*

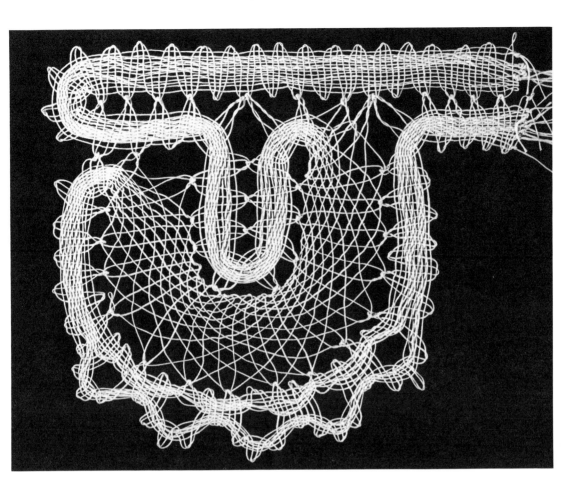

FILLING GROUNDS

At the beginning of its development, Eastern European tape lace was made so dense that no openings remained to be filled. The same thing happened in Italy, where the early Milanese tapes—although less dense—were connected only by braids. Later on, the dense tapes with their heavy feeling gave way to more openly designed tape laces with wide gaps of irregular spaces. Western European lacemakers filled the openings by making the general design of the tape first and then hanging on new pairs of bobbins, which they used to fill the openings with grounds. When a lacemaker finished filling one opening, she either tied the threads off and cut them or led them under the next tape to fill the next opening.

Eastern European lacemak-ers found a different solution for filling the openings between tapes, which I will use in the following samples. Taking into consideration two practical qualities of the tape lace—the facts that the tapes are made with a very small number of bobbins and that the bobbins that form the tape are the only ones to be used, eliminating the need to add or delete bobbins—these lacemakers make their tapes with wide open spaces and fill them with some of the threads from the tape. They usually work one or two pairs of the bobbins back and forth across the empty field and afterwards engage them back in the tape. Thus the field is filled while the tape is being made.

The consecutive rows of the fillings are sewn together, as is the tape framing the opening and the filling. In the latter case, sewing is done by either the tape or the filling, whichever is made last. Usually the leader and the passive pair of bobbins closest to the opening form the filling—thus you hardly notice the bobbins leaving the tape.

The patterns and samples that follow are positioned so you can see the working of the filling ground right-side up. However, the tape that frames the filling must be made first, starting in the lower left-hand corner. Thus, when you begin the tape, you must turn the pattern upside down so the starting point is in the upper right-hand corner. (The pairs are numbered from left to right as usual.) By the time you work the tape to the point where you begin the filling ground, the pattern will be right-side up again.

Sample One. The leader alone forms the filling ground in this sample (see Figures 53 and 54) by working in zigzag lines between the inside edges of the tape in progress and the finished tape. As the leader moves from one pin to another toward the sewing point (on the finished tape), it always twists three times. On the way back to the tape in progress, the leader sews onto those twisted threads when they intersect. When the leader reaches the tape in progress, it works back and forth twice and repeats the sequence just described.

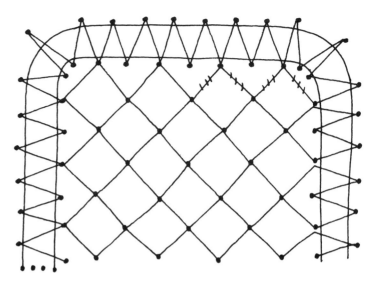

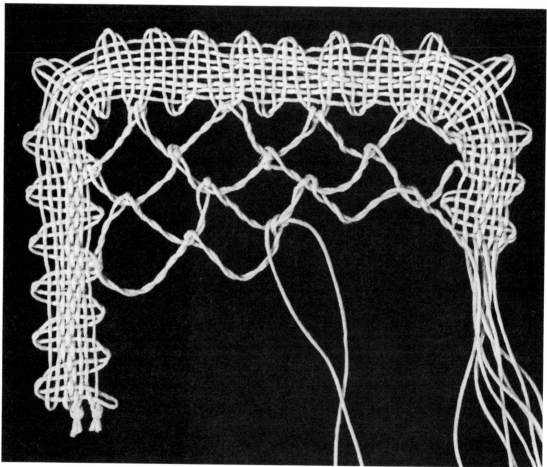

Figure 53. *(Top) Pattern for the first sample—the leader alone makes the entire ground.*

Figure 54. *(Above) Sample One—as you can see, the tape on the right edge is worked along with the rows of ground.*

Sample Two. The same design is used in this sample as in the previous one, but this time the leader and the passive pair of bobbins on the inside edge of the tape make the ground (see Figures 55 and 56). Again the bobbins forming the filling move from pin to pin in zigazg lines, but as they do so they form braids. The braids are used for the entire filling ground and are sewn together where they intersect.

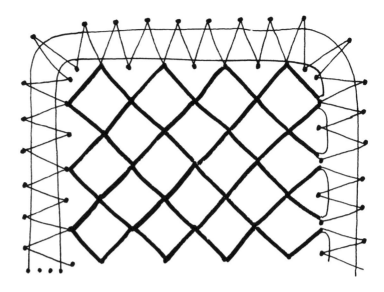

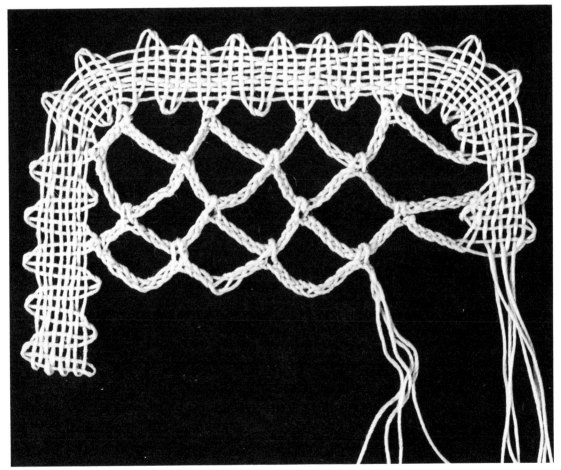

Figure 55. *(Top) The pattern for this sample is the same as the one in Figure 53, except the thicker lines indicate that the filling is a braid rather than a twisting leader.*

Figure 56. *(Above) Sample Two— the braided ground is worked with the leader and the passive pair on the inside edge of the tape.*

Sample Three. This is basically the same lace as in Sample Two, except that lozenges replace the braids (see Figures 57 and 58). The leader and the passive pair on the inside edge of the tape form the lozenges that are held in place by pins. When you do this, plan to make an even number of lozenges in each row. After you complete the first row of lozenges, you sew the last one to the tape on the left. Then you work back to the right, sewing the new lozenges to the ones above where they meet. As you continue, follow the pattern and make sure the lozenges go up and down as illustrated—this is especially important with respect to the structural soundness of the tape on the right.

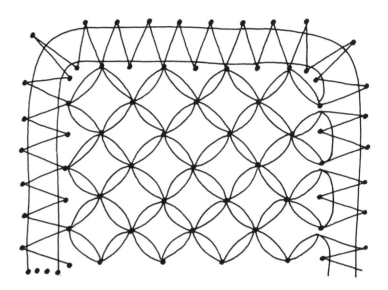

Figure 57. *(Top) Pattern for lace using lozenge leadworks as the ground. Please note that it is important to use an even number of lozenges in each row.*

Figure 58. *(Above) Sample Three— lozenge leadwork produces a ground that is denser and more decorative than the grounds in the first two samples.*

Sample Four. A zigzagging pair of bobbins is used again here, but this time a horizontal pair runs through the zigzag line (see Figures 59 and 60). This not only gives a different appearance to the lace but also lends stabilization to its structure. The leader runs horizontally, while the passive pair at the inside edge of the tape makes the zigzag motion. Where these two pairs meet, they intersect in a whole stitch. Each pair twists two or three times between every two intersections or between an intersection and a pin. These twists are symbolized in the pattern by slashes across the line, each slash indicating where the threads cross.

When the leader reaches the finished tape (on the left side of Figure 60), sew it to the loop of that tape. When the pair moving in the zigzag line works back toward the right, sew it to the previous row of zigzags wherever they meet.

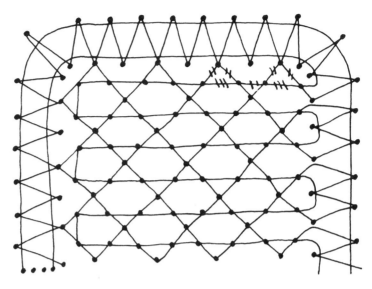

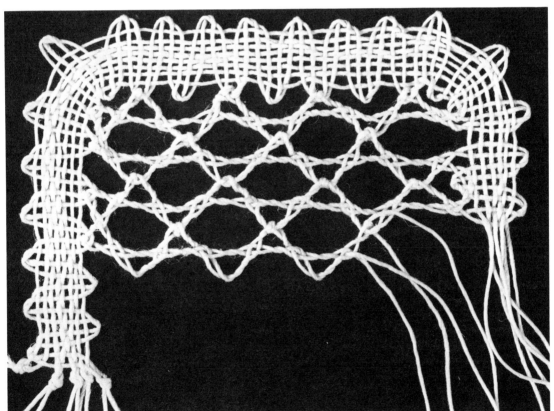

Figure 59. *(Top) This pattern shows a horizontal pair of bobbins running through the zigzag lines made by another pair.*

Figure 60. *(Above) Sample Four— not only is the appearance of this ground different from the ground in Sample One, but it is also stronger structurally.*

Sample Five. The ground in this sample consists of braids made by the leader pair and one passive pair at the inside edge of the tape (see Figures 61 and 62). The braid is made long enough to loop up to the bottom edge of the tape at the top of the sample. There you sew one of the pairs of the braid to a loop in the tape made previously by the leader pair. Then sew that same pair around itself as illustrated in Figure 63. The next step is to join the two pairs together again and repeat the process. On the way back, sew one pair of bobbins forming the braid around the braid in the row above the same way you did in the top row, and then sew that pair around itself. When you reach the tape in progress on the right again, one pair assumes the leader role and works through the tape, while the other pair becomes the passive pair at the inside edge.

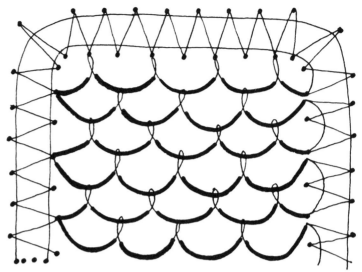

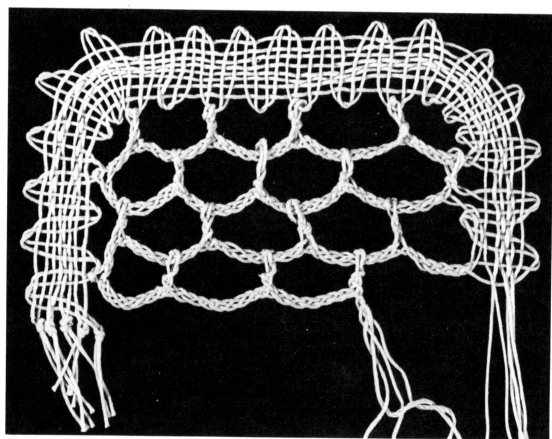

Figure 61. *(Top) Pattern for the fifth sample.*

Figure 62. *(Above) Sample Five—the ground is made by the leader and one passive pair, which form braids long enough to loop up to the row of braids or the tape above.*

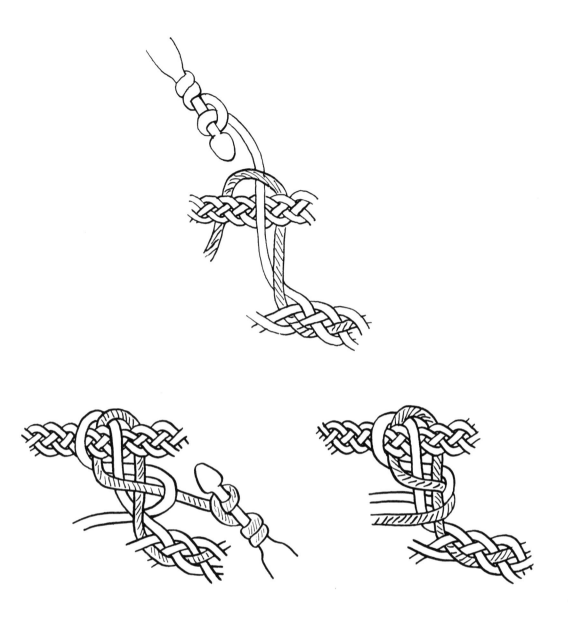

Figure 63. *To sew a braid to a previously made braid or tape: pass one bobbin of one of the pairs of the braid through a loop made by the other thread of the pair (top); sew the same two bobbins around themselves (left); and then (right) join that pair of bobbins with the other pair and work the braid again.*

Sample Six. This is another interesting and effective way to fill a circular opening within a tape (see Figures 64 and 65). Make the tape to the point where the first lozenge leadwork begins, and then form the lozenge leadwork with the leader pair and pair 2. When the shape is finished, turn one pair around a pin placed in the center of the circle. With the same two pairs, form another lozenge leading back to the tape. Before working the pairs that made the lozenges through the tape, go back to where you began the first lozenge. Using pair 3 as the leader, work it through the tape back and forth twice, at which point it again assumes its passive role.

Pair 2 also takes its passive role in the tape again, and the leader pair 1 is worked through the tape back and forth twice. Repeat this entire sequence twice more, so you have a total of six lozenges. After making the fifth lozenge, though, instead of turning one pair around the pin in the center, sew it through the other two loops of the previous lozenges. After making the sixth lozenge, continue making the rest of the tape.

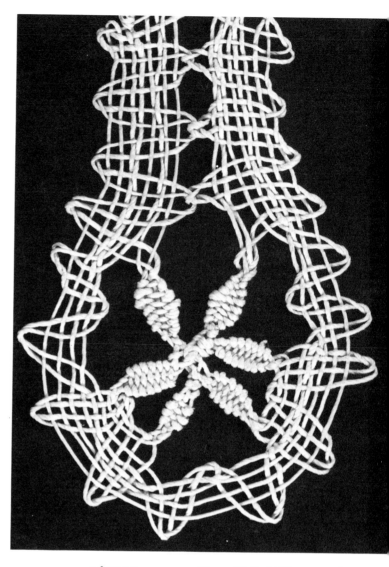

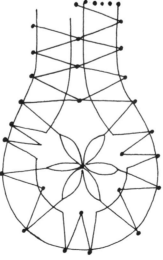

Figure 64. *(Left) The pattern for this sample shows that the passive pair along the inside edge of the tape joins with the leader to form the central lozenge leadworks.*

Figure 65. *(Above) Sample Six—another way to fill a circular opening is with lozenge leadwork, a somewhat more decorative method than the ones described previously.*

COMBINING FILLING GROUNDS

Versatile and interesting tape lace can be made by combining filling grounds. The example that follows integrates filling grounds described in Samples Two and Three (see Figures 56 and 58) and the lozenge rosette illustrated in Sample Six (see Figure 65). The resulting lace can be used either as an insertion or a repeat in an edging (see Figures 66 and 67).

Beginning at point A (in Figure 66), work the tape around to point B. There the leader and pair 2 begin making lozenge leadwork to the left and then back to point B. Continue making the tape to point C, and then begin the ground with the leader and pair 2 again. Start by making a braid, and then alternate braids and lozenges in zigzag rows back and forth to point C. Work the two pairs back into the tape until they come to point D, where again you make two rows of alternating braids and lozenges until you reach point D again.

Continue making the tape all the way to the round opening at the bottom of the motif, where the leader and one passive pair form the petals of the central rosette. After you complete the bottom portion of the motif, work the tape all the way around to point E. Make two rows of the braided ground. When you reach point E again, work the tape to point F, and make two more rows of the braided ground. When you reach point F again, continue to make the tape until point G, where you begin alternating braids and lozenges again. Work the tape and the grounds in the second half of the project in a mirror image of the first half to complete the motif.

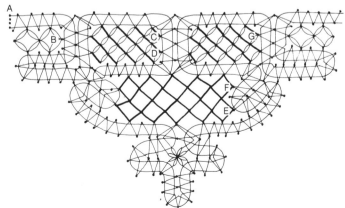

Figure 66. (Left) Only five pairs of bobbins work this entire project, a section of an edging. The pattern shows that the filling grounds described in Figures 56, 58, and 65 are combined here.

Figure 67. (Above) This project illustrates how a complex and intricate lace can be designed from combining filling grounds and simple tapes.

COLOR IN FILLING GROUNDS

Since only a few threads of a tape are used to make the filling ground of a tape lace, it is possible to create grounds of contrasting colors to the tape. There are many ways to do this, and perhaps the simplest is to form a ground from a single twisted pair of bobbins as described in Sample One on page 136. The twisted pair is a gimp in a different color from the rest of the threads running through the tape. When the times comes to form the filling ground, this gimp is led to the inside edge of the tape to form the ground. Thus the entire ground is the color of the gimp, while the tape (aside from the inconspicuous gimp) is of another color.

Another effective way to achieve a different colored ground is by using a lozenge-shaped leadwork ground. Because only one thread does the weaving in making the lozenges, all other threads used in its contstruction are concealed by the weaver. This technical factor opens up many possibilities, including alternating color lozenges.

Sample One. The filling ground of lozenges here is red, contrasting to the white of the tape (see Figures 68 and 69). The red gimp pair runs through the middle of the tape and replaces the leader when it is time to make the lozenges. At that point, you bring the gimp pair to the inside edge of the tape, where it joins with the passive white pair at the inside edge to form the lozenge filling ground.

By choosing one of the red gimp threads to be the weaver, the lozenges will be red.

You could also make the two threads of the gimp different colors, in which case you would have two colors to use for the lozenges. Also, you could make all lozenges within one field of the sample one color and lozenges in the next field a different color.

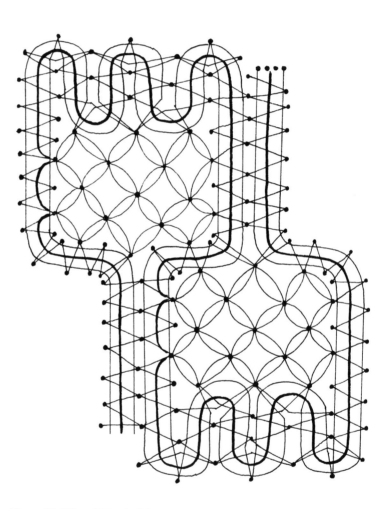

Figure 68. *(Above) The thick line on the pattern represents the gimp pair that replaces one of the white pairs in this sample and forms lozenge leadwork. In this case, the gimp pair is red.*

Figure 69. *(Right) Sample One— leadwork lends itself well to colored grounds since one colored thread acting as the weaver can cover all the other threads in the leadwork.*

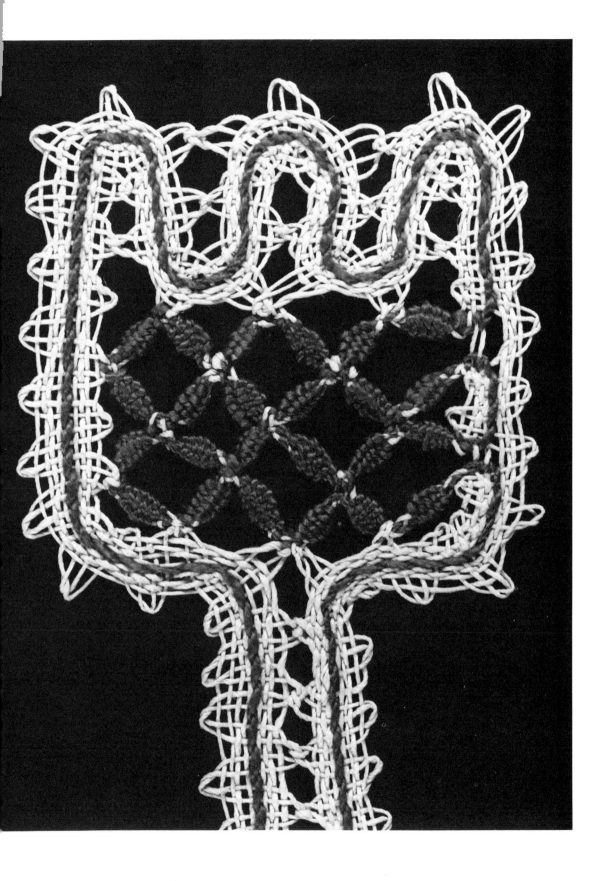

Sample Two. If you want a ground to be a different color from the rest of the tape, you must use two additional pairs of bobbins. The result is a lace that resembles Milanese tape laces but is technically less cumbersome. In this sample, the two sides of the tape are constructed separately (see Figures 70 and 71). After making one repeat of the white tapes, loop the two pairs of bobbins with colored thread over a single pin just to the right of the repeat. Begin making the braided ground as described in Sample Two on page 137. Make rows of this filling ground, sewing it to the tape and to itself at points of intersection. Work the filling ground one step behind the tape to the end of the sample.

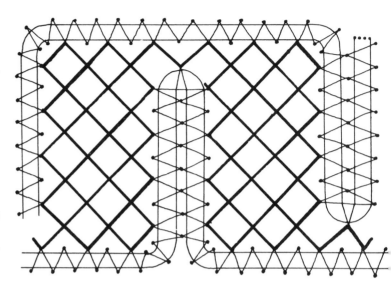

Figure 70. *(Top) The ground, represented by the thick lines, is worked with different bobbins from the tapes.*

Figure 71. *(Above) Sample Two—in order to have colored filling ground without having that color appear in the tapes, you must add the colored threads with more bobbins.*

STARTING AND DISCONTINUING TAPES

In some tape lace designs you have to discontinue and add tapes to the lace, and the project of a bird described here illustrates how to do these things (see Figures 72 and 73). The first step is to outline the body of the bird with a tape started by hanging bobbins over pins in a horizontal line across its width. You work from the bird's lower back just below the tail feathers, and follow the pattern to a point just before the beak. There you begin the eye in lozenge leadwork as described in Sample Six on page 142. Work a loop of two lozenges and hold them in place with a pin. Continue the tape outlining the body to a point at the back of the bird's head, and do the other two lozenge leadworks to complete the eye.

As you go, begin to work the filling ground along with the tape—this filling ground is the one described in Sample Four on page 139. When you reach your original starting point, connect the beginning and end of the tape. Sew each pair of bobbins to its original loop, which was formed when the pair was draped over a pin. After sewing the threads together, tie them in a square knot. Since you are working the bird on the wrong side, these knots will not be noticeable when you turn the lace to its right side.

Next, make the tail of the bird from a separate tape and attach it to the body by sewing each pair of bobbins to a loop on the outside edge (see Figure 74). After making the tail, sew on and tie off the threads as described above.

The tapes that make the crown are handled in a different manner. The five pairs of bobbins that form the first part (on the left) are all hung over one pin at the center of the curl. By working the leader a fewer number of times back and forth in linen stitch, the passive pairs pack very closely together, and this results in a narrow tape. As you go around the curl, work the leader back and forth closer and closer together to widen the tape. When you reach the head, sew the threads to the tape there and tie them off.

The second part of the crown (on the right) is worked in another way to illustrate that there is more than one way to do the same thing. Like the first part, it is worked in linen stitch with five pairs of bobbins, but you start with only three pairs— one leader and two passive. The two remaining pairs are added as shown in Figure 75. After the leader turns at the inner side of the curving tape, the pair to be added and the leader form a linen stitch. The leader then works through the rest of the

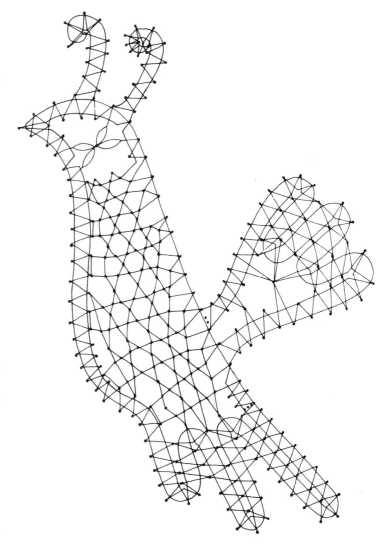

Figure 72. *The pattern for the bird shows that the body is outlined by a tape beginning at the back tail feather and working all the way along the front of the bird to the back of its head where the ground is started. At that point, the ground and tape are worked on at the same time.*

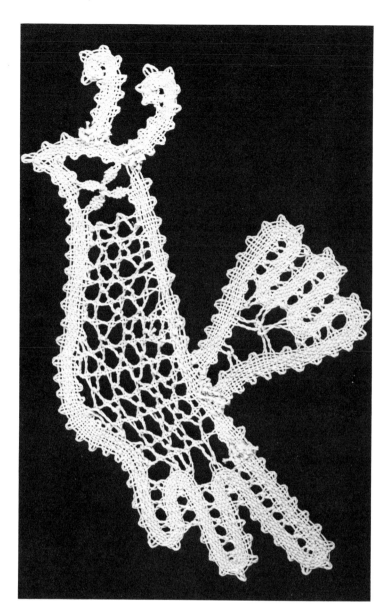

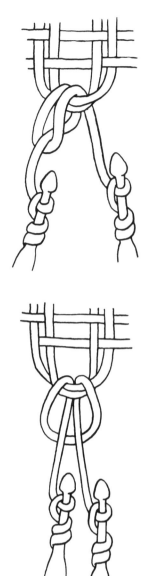

Figure 73. *(Above) Bird lace as seen from the wrong side. The tail and crown are made separately—note how they are attached.*

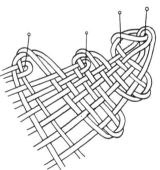

Figure 74. *(Above) Top, one method of attaching a new pair of bobbins to a tape by sewing the pair through an existing loop of the tape. Bottom, an alternate method— pass both bobbins through the loop formed by the new pair. The pairs used to make the tail of the bird are attached to the body in this way.*

Figure 75. *(Left) Additional pairs of bobbins are added in this manner as the curl of the crown in the bird lace widens.*

passive pairs as usual. This method of widening the tape is especially effective when making tapes that vary their width considerably. This tape is connected to the tape forming the bird's head the same way as the first part of the crown.

The finished bird lace (Figure 73) is photographed on the working side (wrong side) to correspond with the working draft and to show how the separate tapes are started, added, and discontinued.

DESIGNING TAPE LACE

Designing tape lace is quite a bit simpler than designing straight lace. For one thing, fewer bobbins are used to work tape lace. Not only is it physically easier to work a handful of bobbins than a few hundred, but the method used to work the bobbins also differs. In tape lace the same few bobbins are worked continuously, winding and weaving about to form the design. In straight lace many bobbins must be worked simultaneously—the continuation of one section of lace depends upon the continuation of an ad-

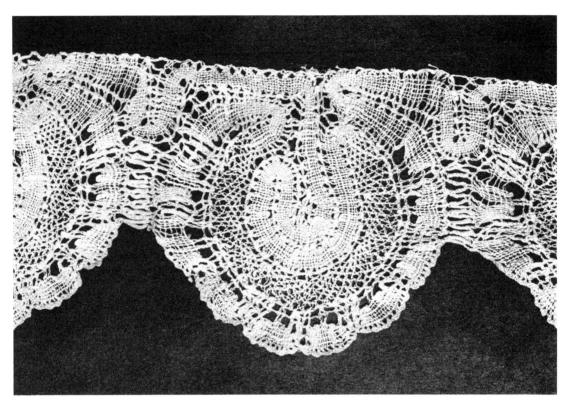

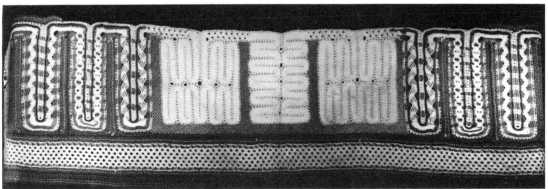

Figure 76. *(Top) Russian tape lace edging. Collection of Ester Oldham, photo by Bill Fuhrmann.*

Figure 77. *(Above) Lace forms a major part of Eastern European traditional costumes—this portion of Slovakian lace from a woman's hat is an example. Collection of the U.L.U.V. Bratislava, photo by S. Stepanek, courtesy Ema Markova.*

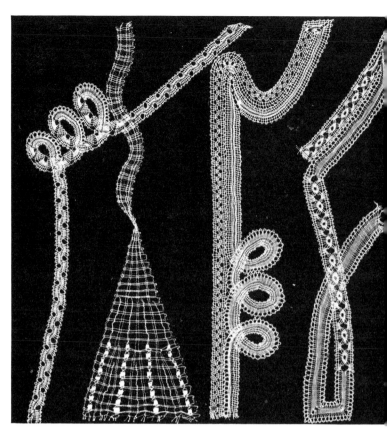

Figure 78. *Free-form tapes in this* Small Flat Composition *by Elena Holeczy. The tapes are made from white linen thread and silver threads. Photo Pavel Janek.*

Figure 79. *Handspun hemp and linen thread in natural colors and gold thread form Elena Holeczy's composition* Hey Horses, My Black Horses, *made in 1969–1970 (detail). Photo Pavel Janek.*

jacent section—and this requires more planning of the design in advance. In tape lace, although there is a need for some planning in advance, you are freer to design as you go. The transition from tape to ground or from stitch to stitch is also easier in tape lace.

If the tapes are constructed so they are structurally sound, proportionately larger openings can be left between the tapes without weakening the lace. As a matter of fact, a well-constructed tape lace is very strong and durable and holds its shape well. Tape laces with heavily scalloped edges take advantage of this. Also, because you are working with relatively few bobbins, laces of virtually unlimited size are possible. For the same reason, the overall shape of the lace can range from geometric to highly irregular.

The success of your designs for either type of lace depends on how well you adapt your ideas to the type of lace best suited to your objectives. Making the transition from the tape lace samples just described to major tape lace pieces of your own design is probably best accomplished by following the same basic procedures outlined on pages 102–105 for straight lace.

First, design your own sample, varying the stitches of the tape and grounds, the spaces between them, and the direction of the tape. It would be best to plan the entire lace in advance and repeat the same motif to limit your variables (see Figures 76 and 77 for traditional designs with a repeating motif).

The next step in designing may take many forms. You can design another sample with changing motifs that create interest by their uniqueness and variety (see Figure 78). Or you may wish to simply pin some bobbins on your pillow and

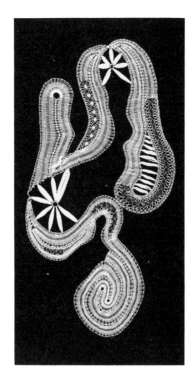

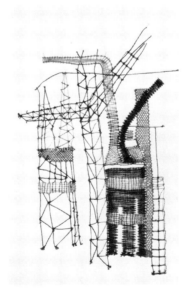

Figure 80. *(Top) Free-form tape lace, 20½" x 11"/520mm x 280mm. Elena Holeczy made this piece entitled* Flat Composition Within a Rectangular Space, No. 2 *in white linen thread and gold thread in 1967. Photo Pavel Janek.*

Figure 81. *(Above) Free-form lace study by Eva Proskova that combines tape lace and straight lace. Courtesy Jarmila Sikytova, photo V.S.U.P.*

create a composition with a tape as you work, changing the stitches and direction of the tape, creating different filling grounds, crossing the tape, and so forth. The end result may simply be a sample, a study, or a finished composition (see Figure 80). You can combine these two methods by making a composition of free tapes either entirely or partially planned in advance to vary all the aspects—the stitches and grounds, the direction of the tape, the motifs, and the shapes created by the outlining tapes.

After you experiment, you will have a much better idea of what you can do with tape lace, and you will develop the ability to create your own designs. At this point, you should consolidate what you have learned by making some definite pieces. The many historical and contemporary examples of tape laces illustrating this book can show you what other lacemakers have done. Keep in mind that some very successful laces can be made by combining tape lace and straight lace (see Figure 81)—and this opens up many possibilities for you to explore. You can work these combination laces separately and connect them by crochetage or begin with several tapes that merge together to form straight lace and later separate back to form individual tapes.

Another area to explore is using color in tape lace (see Figure 79). When you start to do this, confine the use of one or two colors to within the tape before you lead it out into the grounds. The use of color will naturally lead you to the exploration of other materials and objects to combine with the lace.

If you follow this suggested sequence of exploration and study your results, you will be able to make laces that truly express your ideas and feelings.

FINISHING UP

In this section I discuss solutions to the more common situations you may encounter as you make lace. They mainly deal with finishing lace, attaching laces to other materials, and handling completed laces. If you come across any situations that are not discussed here, apply the basic principles you learned in this book, and you should be able to solve any problems.

FINISHING ENDS OF LACE

The way in which the threads are handled once the lace is finished depends upon how the lace is going to be used. If you are making long, narrow strips of lace that are going to be cut into shorter lengths for a particular use, you do not have to finish off the ends at all. If, on the other hand, you intend to use the piece as a whole, there are a few methods you can use to finish the ends. One method is to tie the pairs off in a square knot after you work the last row (see Figure 1). You should do this while the bobbins are still attached to the threads to make the process easier. Make the knots right up against the lace, but be careful not to compress the stitches by pulling too hard on the threads in the process.

Another method of finishing

Ballet by Elena Holeczy, detail. Straight and tape lace made of white and silver threads.

the ends that is especially useful when you plan to leave a fringe (see Figure 2) is to tie the pairs of threads off by an overhand knot (see Figure 3). Again, leave the bobbins on the threads until you complete the knot. This knot requires a little more care to position, and therefore it is best to tighten it gradually as you work it into its proper place. The threads are usually tied off in pairs, but in the case of the table runner pictured in Figure 48 on pages 88–89, each overhand knot is made with two pairs to give the fringe more body.

If you do not want knots or fringe on the end of the lace, you can make the end look like the beginning. Tie the ends off in square knots, always in pairs as usual. With the wrong side of the lace facing you, bring each pair back onto the lace and sew it to the back no further than ½″/15mm from the edge (see Figure 4). Naturally, you should choose places in the lace that are dense, so the threads will not show from the front once the lace is turned over. Pull on the pairs just enough to make a neat edge, secure them by tying the threads in a square knot once more, and trim the ends so they are about ¼″/7mm long. Repeat this procedure until all of the pairs are sewn to the back edge of the lace. If you work carefully, the result is a neat and clean edge.

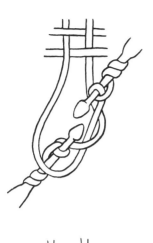

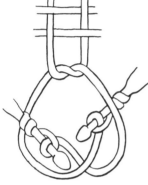

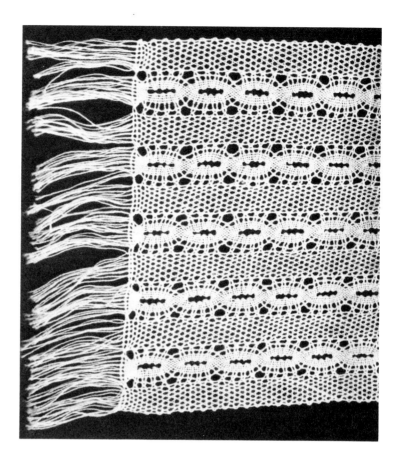

Figure 1. *(Above) Making the square knot to finish the lace: top, the left bobbin passes through the loop from the back; bottom, that same bobbin passes through the loop from the top and the knot is secured against the edge of the lace.*

Figure 2. *(Above right) Contemporary scarf made in the U.S.S.R. Manmade fiber threads are worked in the tape lace techniques. Collection of Mary Lou Reichard, photo Howard J. Levitz.*

Figure 3. *(Right) The overhand knot to finish the lace.*

Figure 4. *(Below right) Concealing thread ends. Left, the threads are tied in a square knot at the edge of the lace. Middle, the threads are sewn to the lace about ½"/15mm back from the edge. Right, the threads are secured by tying another square knot and cutting off the excess thread. Please note that this drawing shows the lace as viewed from the wrong side.*

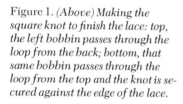

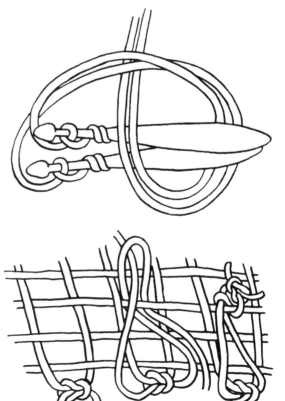

ATTACHING LACE TO OTHER MATERIALS

Lace is combined very often with other materials, especially in household linens and clothing. You can use lace as an edging and attach it to the edge of a fabric both to decorate the material and also to keep the edge of the fabric from becoming worn. Or you can appliqué lace to a fabric, letting the fabric show through the lace. Lace can also be used as an insertion and put into openings in the fabric. In all of these cases you must attach the lace to the fabric securely and neatly. In cases such as edgings, collars, and cuffs, the attached lace has to be able to be removed easily for separate laundering.

Edgings and Insertions. To attach an edging or insertion to fabric, first make a hem as wide or narrow as is appropriate along the edge of that fabric. Then sew the edging to the fabric with a whipping stitch, always catching the extreme edge of the lace edging and the extreme edge of the hem at regular intervals (see Figure 5). Usually the thread used should be the same color as the lace, and the needle should be fine and sharp to prevent its pulling either the fabric or the lace.

One variation of this method is to overlap the edge of the hemmed fabric with the lace. The amount of overlap depends on the design of the edging and your personal taste, but usually the lace overlaps no more than one-quarter of its width. Lace attached this way is sewn to the fabric with a sewing machine or by hand using a back stitch (see Figure 6).

The reverse of the method just described makes a handsome attachment also. The fabric slightly overlaps the lace so the lace seems to be coming from underneath the fabric (see

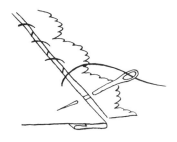

Figure 5. *A lace edging sewn to a hemmed fabric by a whipping stitch, catching the extreme edges of the fabric and the lace.*

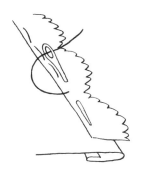

Figure 6. *Another way to attach a lace edging (or insertion) to a hemmed fabric is to overlap the fabric with the lace and sew by hand using a back stitch.*

Figure 7. *Attaching the fabric to the lace by slightly overlapping the lace with the fabric.*

Figure 7). To do this, turn the fabric over after making the hem and place the lace on the hem so it slightly overlaps the fabric. Sew the lace to the fabric with either a whipping stitch or a back stitch in regular intervals. Be careful not to go through more than one thickness of fabric with the needle so the stitches do not show on the right side of the fabric.

To create a stronger, more durable connection between the fabric and lace, while still having the lace look like it comes from underneath the fabric, begin by laying the fabric down, right side up. Next, place the lace right side down on the fabric so the foot of the lace is even with the edge of the fabric. Carefully place a strip of hem binding face down on top of the lace, even with the edges of both the lace and the fabric (see Figure 8). Using a sewing machine (or by hand if you prefer), sew all three pieces of material together a short distance from the edge. Then, turn the hem under and sew it to the wrong side of the fabric (see Figure 8). The lace, secured between the fabric and the hem binding, will stick out.

All of these methods can be applied when you want to attach insertions to a fabric. The difference is, of course, that you sew both edges of the lace to the fabric instead of just one.

Appliqué and Inlay. A very effective use of lace is as an appliqué upon another net or solid fabric or as an inlay set into a fabric. Usually, when the pieces of lace are small, the net or fabric is not cut away behind the lace and this is known as true lace appliqué. When the lace is large and a transparent feeling is desired, the fabric behind the lace is cut away and the technique is called inlay rather than appliqué.

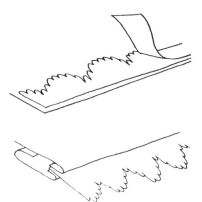

Figure 8. *Another stronger, way of attaching fabric to lace. Top, you lay the fabric down right side up place the lace on the fabric right side down so the foot of the lace is even with the edge of the fabric, and lay the hem binding on top of the lace even with the edge. Sew all of these pieces together a short distance from the edge. Bottom, turn the hem binding under and sew it to the fabric.*

Regardless of which technique you decide to use, begin by attaching the lace to the fabric. Both the material and the lace should be flat, without creases, and have straight edges. Do not stretch the material into a frame or hoop because after you sew on the lace and take the material off the hoop, the tension will be relieved and the lace will pucker. To sew on the lace, the best thing to do first is to baste the lace through its center and along its edges to the material. Once the lace is held in place this way, you can sew it easily and permanently to the fabric with small, regularly spaced whipping stitches. It is a good idea to use sewing thread that is about the same color and thickness as that used in making the lace.

Although the method just described is a very satisfactory one for appliquéd laces, it is not good enough for inlaid laces because the raw edges of the cut fabric would unravel. For inlaid laces you can use a closely sewn satin stitch or buttonhole stitch to bind the edges of the cut fabric. Or you can sew the lace with small whipping stitches and cut the fabric, leaving about ¼"/7mm extra along the edges. Roll the material back to form a rolled hem, and then sew the roll to the back of the fabric with small whipping stitches.

CARE OF LACE

If you have a precious old lace that needs refurbishing, I suggest you take it to a professional cleaner specializing in restoring old laces. The most reputable professional lace cleaners I know of is the Unique and Art Lace Cleaners in St. Louis, Missouri. (See *Supplies and Suppliers* at the end of the book.) For most other laces, just launder them following a few simple directions.

If possible, use soft water and a low-sudsing, mild detergent.

The temperature of the water depends upon the material in the lace. For example, linen and cotton laces should be laundered in boiling water, while silk and woolen laces—which would be damaged if exposed to such temperatures—must be laundered in lukewarm water. Stir the lace in the solution—do not rub, since rubbing may cause the surface of the threads to become frayed and rough. After washing, rinse the lace several times, changing the water after each rinsing.

Linen does not require starching, but you may wish to starch laces made of other materials. If so, the best starch to use is the old-fashioned, boiled starch, because it penetrates the fibers far deeper than spray starch. Once the starch is boiled, you can use it at any temperature. Remember to starch the lace only after it has been thoroughly rinsed. Avoid bleach—if you must use it to whiten a lace yellowed with age, use it sparingly and rinse the lace thoroughly afterwards.

After the lace has been rinsed or starched, dry it by laying it flat and stretching it to its original size and shape on a soft board covered with several thicknesses of clean white fabric. It is a good idea to pin it down in several places with pins that will not rust. Do not iron the lace—ironing has a tendency to catch the lace, pulling it out of shape.

Lace, of course, lasts longest when it is being used. But if you must store it, store it flat or rolled on a paper roll. Never fold lace, as the creases may become permanent and will cause the fibers at the fold to weaken and deteriorate more rapidly than the rest of the fibers in the lace. White laces should be covered while in storage with non-acidic tissue paper to prevent yellowing.

BIBLIOGRAPHY

Bamateanu, T., Fosca, G., and Ionescu, E. *Folk Costumes of Rumania*. Rumania: State Publishing House for Literature and the Arts, c. 1958

Bath, Virginia Churchill. *Lace*. Chicago: Regnery, c. 1974

———. *Barbour's Prize Needlework Series*, Nos. 3 and 4. Barbour Brothers Company, c. 1895

Bossert, H. *Peasant Art in Europe*. Berlin: Ernst Wasmuth, c. 1926

Butnik-Siberskiy, B. *Ukrainske Narodne Mistetsvo*. Kiev: "Mistetsvo," c. 1967

Caufield, S. F. A., and Seward, Blanche C. *Dictionary of Needlework*. London: W. Cowan

Channer, C. C. *Lacemaking, Point Ground*. Leicester: The Dryard Press, c. 1970

Czarnecka, Irena. *Polnische Volkskunst*. Poland: Warsava, c. 1957

Davydova, S. *Russkoe Kruzevo and Russkie Kruzevnicy*, Vols. 1 and 2. St. Petersburg, c. 1892

de Dillmont, Therese. *Encyclopedia of Needlework*, Mulhouse, France: D.M.C. Library

Editors of American Fabrics Magazine. *Encyclopedia of Textiles*. New Jersey: Prentice Hall, c. 1960

Emery, Irene. *The Primary Structures of Fabrics*. Washington, D. C.: Textile Museum, c. 1966

Fel, E., Hofer, T., and Csillery, K. *Hungarian Peasant Art*. Budapest: Corvina, c. 1958

Gorbunoff, M. *Uber Russische Spitzenindustries*. Vienna, c. 1886

Grom, Bogdan. *Slovene Ornaments*. Trieste: Folcloristic Collection, c. 1949

Gubser, Elsie H. *Bobbin Lace*. Oregon: Robin and Russ Handweavers, c. 1975

Gyula, Ortutay. *A Magyar Nepmuveszet*. Kiadasa: Franklin-Tarsulat, c. 1941

Jackson, Emily F. *A History of Handmade Lace*. New York: Charles Scribner's Sons, c. 1900

Kaminska, Janina, and Turnau, Irene. *Zarys Historii Wlokiennictva Na Zemiach Polskich*. Wroclaw, c. 1966

Kovacevicova, Sona. *Lidove Vytvarne Umeni*. Czechoslovakia: Statni Pedagogicke Nakladatelstvi, c. 1974

Kybalova, Ludmila. *Emilie Palickova Bibliography*. Czechoslovakia: Nakladatelstvi Ceskoslovenskzch Vytvarnych Umelcu, c. 1962

Loukomski, G. K. *Le Kreml De Moscou*. Paris: Editions Milsson, c. 1927

Lowes, Emily Leigh. *Chats on Old Lace and Needlework*. London: T. Fisher Unwin, c. 1908

Maidment, Margaret. *Manual of Handmade Bobbin Lacework*. Chicheley, England: Paul P. B. Minet, c. 1971

Makovski, S. *Peasant Art of Subcarpathian Russia*, Czechoslovakia: Plamja, c. 1926

Markova, Ema. *Slovenske Cipky*. Bratislava, Czechoslovakia: Slovenske Vydavatelstvo Krasnej Literatury, c. 1962

Mayer, Christa. "Three Centuries of Bobbin Lace." *Antiques Magazine*, August, 1966

Mincoff, Elizabeth, and Marriage, Margaret S. *Pillow Lace—A Practical Handbook*. Chicheley, England: Paul P.B. Minet, c. 1971

Oprescu, George. *"Peasant Art in Roumania."* Special 1929 Autumn issue of *Creative Art*. New York: Albert and Charles Boni

Palliser, Mrs. Bury. *A History of Lace*. London: Low and Searle, c. 1875

Patkova, Jarmila. *Ludovy Odev V Okoli Trnavy*. Bratislava, Czechoslovakia: Slovenske Vydavatelstvo Krasnej Literatury, c. 1957

Pietkewicz, Kazimier. *Haft I Zdobenie Stroju Ludovego*. Warszawa: Sztuka, c. 1955

Pond, Gabrielle. *An Introduction to Lace.* New York: Charles Scribner's Sons, c. 1973

Rabotova, I. P. *Russkoe Narodnoe Kruzevo.* Moscow, USSR: Vsesouznoe Kooperativnoe Izdashcelstvo, c. 1956

Schuette, Marie. *Alte Spitzen.* Richard Carl Schmidt and Co., c. 1914

Sharp, Mary. *Point and Pillow Lace.* New York: E. P. Dutton and Co., c. 1913

Slassoff, W. *L'Ornament National Russe.* St. Petersburg, c. 1872

Stech, V. V., and Vydrova, J. *Kouzlo Bilych Niti.* Hradec Kralove, Czechoslovakia: Krajska Gallerie, c. 1965

Tebbs, Lousia A. *The Art of Bobbin Lace.* Chicheley, England: Paul P. B. Minet, c. 1972

Vaclavik, Antonin, and Orel, Jaroslav. *Texile Folk Art.* Czechoslovakia: Artia Praha, c. 1956

Von Henneberg, Freiherr Alfred. *The Art and Craft of Old Lace.* New York: E. Weyhe, c. 1931

Whiting, Gertrude. *Old Time Tools and Toys of Needlework.* New York: Dover Publication, c. 1971

———. *A Lace Guide for Makers and Collectors.* New York: E. P. Dutton and Co., c. 1920

Supplies and Suppliers

Berga-Ullman, Inc.
P. O. Box 918
North Adams, Massachusetts 01247
All supplies

E. Braggings and Sons, Ltd.
26–36 Silver Street
Bedford, England
All supplies

Janet and John Crouch
Oak Lodge
47a Morning Road
Woodford Green
Essex, England
Lace books, antique bobbins

Frederick J. Fawcett
129 South Street
Boston, Massachusetts 02130
*Large selection of
linen yarns and threads*

Osma G. Tod Studio
319 Mendoza Avenue
Coral Gables, Florida 33134
Books, instructions, all supplies

Robin and Russ Handweavers
533 N. Adams Street
McMinnville, Oregon 97128
Books, all supplies

Some Place
2990 Adeline Street
Berkeley, California 94703
Books, instructions, all supplies

Textile Studios, Inc.
Windsor Mill
121 Union Street
North Adams, Massachusetts 01247
*Large selection of metallic
and silk threads*

The Unique and Art Lace
Cleaners
5926 Delmar Boulevard
St. Louis, Missouri 63112
*Professional lace cleaning
and restoration*

INDEX

Edited by Ellen Zeifer
Designed by Bob Fillie
Photographs by Howard J. Levitz except where noted
Composed in 10 point Laurel by Publishers Graphics, Inc.
Printed and bound by Interstate Book Manufacturers